An All-Access Tour of the
OLD TESTAMENT

BACKSTAGE PASS
to the Bible

Backstage Pass to the Bible: an all-access tour of the Old Testament

Copyright © 2000 by CWR Production, P.O. Box 230, Farnham, Surrey, GU9 8XG, England.

Youth Specialties Books, 300 S. Pierce St., El Cajon, CA 92020, are published by Zondervan, 5300 Patterson Ave. S.E., Grand Rapids, MI 49530.

Library of Congress Cataloging-in-Publication Data

Brant, Jonathan, 1970-
    Backstage Pass to the Bible : an all-access tour of the Old Testament
/ Jonathan Brant.
      p. cm.
    "Youth Specialties."
    ISBN 0-310-24925-2 (pbk. : alk. paper)
    1. Bible. O.T.—Introductions. I. Title.

BS1140.2 .B73 2000
221.6'1—dc21

99-055173

Edited by Andrew Wooding, Vicki Newby, Tim McLaughlin, Linnea Lagerquist and Rick Marschall
Cover and interior design by David Folkman/Larry Brown Graphic Design
Illustrations by David Yapp
Additional research and concepts contributed by Tricia Brant and Jim Hancock
Production Assistance by Sarah Sheerin and Nicole Davis
Formally published as Downloading the Bible: A Rough Guide to the Old Testament

Printed in the United States of America

02 03 04 05 06 07 08 / CH / 10 9 8 7 6 5 4 3 2

An All-Access Tour of the
OLD TESTAMENT

BACKSTAGE PASS
to the Bible

Youth Specialties

ZONDERVAN™

WWW.ZONDERVAN.COM

Jonathan **Brant**

Contents

Why should i waste my valuable time reading this book?

Why should i waste my valuable time reading this book?

Do you have cable TV or a satellite dish? At first it's so exciting: "Oh boy! There are 24 hours a day of Hungarian soaps on channel 307 and a nail-bitingly exciting armadillo-tossing contest on the sports channel!"

Soon, though, you come to realize the really good programs are on premium channels, and you have to pay extra for a decoder if you want to watch them.

I once lived with a family who had cable TV, and sometimes, when I became bored with the armadillo toss, I would try to watch the special channels. Even without a decoder it was almost possible to tell what's going on.

"Yep, that's definitely basketball. Oh, no wait, it could be the new Eddie Murphy film." Occasionally there's even a moment of total and beautiful clarity: "That's not Eddie Murphy—it's the Queen of England!"

But generally I was peering through a thick fog, the characters' feet at the top of the screen, their heads at the bottom, and thick wavy lines running all through the middle. A less than satisfying viewing experience.

Unfortunately, reading the Bible can be a lot like watching cable TV without a decoder. The story, or the teaching, seems to appear and disappear through a thick fog. We think we know what's going on, but to be honest we're not quite sure. The characters seem upside down and incomprehensible, and what on earth does all this have to do with us anyway?

Still, we plow on (if we have the strength), waiting for that one moment of beautiful clarity when God speaks to us through a particular word or verse—then we plunge back into the fog. Nobody wants that.

So, we present this little book—our version of a decoder—to help you tune in when you read the Bible.

But why should I need a decoder?

Maybe you're saying, "But if the Bible is God's Word, won't the Holy Spirit decode it for me? Why do I need a book to help?"

It's a fair question. There are moments of total, beautiful clarity, no doubt. But God also expects us to expend a little effort ourselves. That's part of God's plan for us.

Here's something to think about. If you traveled back in time just 10 years ago, when I was in school, much of the playground conversation would be completely unintelligible.

Think of slang—would you be insulted or pleased to be called an "Alpha Geek" or a "Mod"? What about TV programs—could you discuss the plot of "Dallas" or laugh at jokes about the Fonz in "Happy Days"? Was "Adam Ant" a kiddie creation like Scooby Doo or a famous singer?

Even in the space of 10 years, people's lifestyles and interests change significantly. So it's interesting to remember the most recent parts of the Bible were written *2,000* years ago. But don't worry. God is not disconnected from all this. God made sure that even though it was written in different languages from ours, by people who never dreamt of cars or factories—let alone computers, modems, or space travel—we can still understand much of what the Bible is about. With a little effort, we can understand *much* more.

It's particularly useful to know how the people of the Bible lived, what they liked and disliked, what they cared about, and what scared them.

And once we know something about when and why a particular book of the Bible was written, what we read will make much more sense.

So, whadaya think? Is it worth the effort to understand? Read on…

So how do I use this book, anyway?

I had a friend who was a genius at math and science but dumb as dirt in English. He failed English three times. We'll never know if he really passed or if they just took pity and let him slide.

One reason he kept failing was he insisted his best chance of getting through was to memorize whole chunks from *Cliffs Notes*. When he walked into an exam, his brain was bursting with a memorized beginning and ending of a story (he just had to fill in the middle). It never occurred to him his teacher might be clever enough to recognize *Cliffs Notes*, or that—call me crazy—it would a better use of his time to just sit down and *read* one of the books.

Sure, fine, make fun of my friend. But understand this: his approach to learning English wasn't much different from the way a lot of people approach the Bible. We like Bible study books but don't get around to actually reading the Bible. Maybe that's slightly better than nothing. But wouldn't it be ever so slightly better to go straight to the source?

Some things were just made to go together: Big Macs and fries, Tom and Jerry, this book and the Bible! Ideally, you should read with this book in one hand and the Bible in the other. The whole idea is to help you understand the Bible better and learn more about what God is saying through it as you read.

Actually, it's a two-way street. You can start by reading the Bible and then come here for more background information. Or you can drive in the other direction, starting with this book and then looking up the parts it recommends in the Bible.

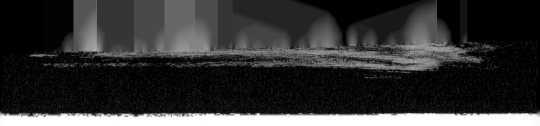

The components of this book

Each book of the Old Testament is covered in *this* book, so whatever you're looking for is listed by page number in the table of contents on page 4.

Most of the books are covered in the order they appear in your Bible, but not all. So don't panic if you can't find one in its usual place—it's in there somewhere. To help out, there's an alphabetical listing on page 108.

The books are dealt with in groups that make them easier to understand—for example, all the prophetic books together and all the historical books together. At the beginning of each section there's a general introduction that gives an idea of the kind of books you're reading.

Once you get into the individual books, you'll find a number of different paragraphs. Here's what you'll find under each heading:

First off...

Like the blurb on the back of a book or video, here's where you get an idea of what the book is about, and how dramatic, amazing, human, bizarre, or intriguing the book is—so you can't keep from reading more!

Ground covered

Maps come in different scales—some cover a few miles in intense detail; others cover the whole world. **Ground covered** is like a global map—the entire book reduced to a postage stamp! In a few words it tells you what's going on in the book as a whole.

Maps in different scales

Main theme

If you've read the Bible quite often, you know that sometimes it's difficult to see the forest for the trees. You think, "What on earth does this mean? And what does it have to do with anything? Why is this story here at all?" Some books in the Bible are so long and cover so many different stories and topics that it's impossible to guess at the overall message.

The **Main theme** paragraphs sums up what you might learn from the book if you had the time and energy to read the whole thing from cover to cover in one shot.

You can then keep this in mind as you read bits of it and see where individual stories fit into the overall message.

But what about me?

At school it's easier to enjoy a subject when you can see how it will help you in life. Physics becomes exciting if you want to work for NASA. If, however, your dream is to be a fashion designer, then the conductivity coefficient of plastic doesn't hold many thrills.

The **But what about me?** section shows how each book in the Bible has important lessons for today. After you've read it you should be better able to apply the contents of the book to your own life and situation. This will make what you're reading more exciting.

glows in the dark!

New plug-in rain coat

Interesting bits
and
Central characters

This is possibly the most important and helpful information of all because it will help you pick up the Bible and explore new territory. These lists will lead you through the minefield of difficult or confusing parts into the heart of the book you're reading. If there's a person you're especially interested in or a story you particularly want to read, you'll probably find it listed here.

Many of the passages listed cover the bits and characters I've underlined in my own Bible in the

past. **interesting bits** and **Central characters** are appetizers and don't include every important event or character. As you read, you can add your own interesting bits and characters to the list.

A few clues about reading the Bible

Little and often

Some restaurants promise if you can eat your way through the entire menu, you eat for free. For snakes (who can eat a huge meal and then digest it for weeks afterwards) that would be a great way to live—slither in once a month and then slide (rather more slowly) home to digest all that free food. But that's not how we humans work. We must eat little and often.

It's the same with Bible reading. What we need is to dip into the Bible as often as possible but not wear ourselves out by doing too much at once. Why not set modest goals for reading the Bible and see what God might do to help you meet them? Don't worry if you don't stick to your plan perfectly; slow and steady wins the race. Try to keep going—or try something fresh if what you're doing isn't working. Do anything, just don't stop!

Read past, present, and future

I want to recommend a time traveler's way of reading the Bible, which will hopefully make it easier to understand and apply to your life. When you read a few verses in the Bible and want to know what they mean to you, try this approach:

Past—Ask yourself questions about when the verses were originally written. What was going on in Israel's history for instance? Then ask yourself: "What might the author have been trying to communicate about God to the people who first read this book?" The **Main theme** section can help you here.

Present—Next, ask yourself what the verses could mean to you today. The **But what about me?** section might be helpful with this part.

Future—Finally, ask yourself: "What am I going to do or think differently in the future in light of what these verses say to me?"

Reading the Bible this way invites God to speak to us and, more importantly, puts us in a position to act on what we hear God saying.

What's so special about the Bible?

What's so special about the Bible?

Danger: Creative genius at work!

Can you imagine living in a monochromatic world? A universe with only one color?

Fortunately, the God who created the universe is a genius. Our world is not black and white but an incredible, multicolor paradise. The latest computer printers and monitors claim to be able to reproduce millions of colors. Impressive—but only a fraction of the colors God used to paint the world.

God went wild! Like some sort of mad professor, he was never content with just doing the job—it had to be fantastic, beautiful, outrageous, and extreme.

Just think of all the different tastes, different animals, different landscapes, different smells—and compare Adam Sandler with Neve Campbell. The world is full of the weird and the wonderful!

Let me introduce myself

Just imagine that the incredible, creative genius wanted to tell you about himself and give you some clues about his creation—your home planet. Imagine he decided to communicate to you through a book. Would he write a boring book? Not! The Bible, God's most specific and detailed way of revealing himself to us, is like the world we live in: a work of genius.

What will I find in the Bible?

The Bible is chock-full of the mysterious and the bizarre.

If the FBI had been around when the Bible was being written, Mulder and Scully would have been run ragged investigating X-file after X-file: a talking donkey, a disembodied finger appearing to write cryptic graffiti on the wall at a king's banquet, and the awesome teacher and prophet who turned water to wine and multiplied a kid's lunch to feed thousands.

But it's not all the stuff of tabloid news headlines. The Bible tells epic tales of war and bloodthirsty battle. Romantic heroes are everywhere: a brave boy defeats a terrible giant, wise leaders save their countries from destruction, beautiful women risk everything to change the course of history, true friends risk their lives to help each other.

But there is a problem

As you read this you might be thinking, "Well, if the Bible is so popular and so exciting, how come I find it so hard to read and understand?"

Fair question. The truth is, the Bible is far more exciting and interesting than a simple textbook, but it takes more effort to understand. Like most things, the more you put in, the more you get out. As any football lover knows, winning seasons require careful planning and disciplined effort—just passing a ball around won't cut it. In the same way we need to find out something about the background of the various parts of the Bible to fully understand and enjoy it.

Turn the page for basic information about the Bible as a whole.

Can we turn on the light?

No, I want to use my new flashlight

The X Files

That big black book on your shelf

If you were to pull down a Bible from your shelf, you'd find it's not just a continuous stream of words—which is good because, taken together, it's one long, long book. There are over 750,000 words, which is equal to more than 20 ordinary novels. I'm happy to report the Bible is divided very sensibly.

The first and biggest division is between the two **testaments**. As you probably know these are called the **Old Testament** and the **New Testament**. The word *testament* means agreement or relationship.

The Old Testament is about the agreement that God made with the ancient nation of Israel.

The New Testament is about the fresh agreement God made with all people through Jesus Christ.

Each testament is then broken down into separate **books**—39 in the old and 27 in the new.

There are two more divisions, which make it much easier to find particular sections. They are the divisions of the books into **chapters** and **verses**. These weren't put there by the authors—they were added much later when people began to print the Bible in large numbers.

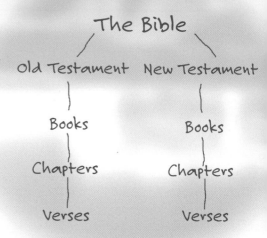

But who wrote all those books?

If God ran an employment agency, it's safe to say he would hire some interesting people. God obviously has his own ideas about what qualifies someone to do a certain job. I imagine if we wanted someone to write books for us, we would probably choose people with degrees in English or journalism.

But the people God "employed" to write his book were from all different walks of life. Some, like Moses and Paul, were highly educated scholars. Some were professionally religious—priests and prophets like Jeremiah and Ezekiel. Still others were normal, working folk: fishermen like Peter, doctors like Luke, farmers like Amos. God even chose a couple of kings, David and Solomon, to have a hand in writing his book.

So it's not really God's book at all then?

Some things in life will always remain mysteries. Why are dinosaurs extinct? Why do we suffer some form of instantaneous brain freeze when we try to make small talk with desirable members of the opposite sex? And how, exactly, did God inspire the writers of the Bible?

We'll probably never understand. Second Timothy 3:16 declares that God was involved in its writing, saying, "All Scripture is God-breathed"—but that doesn't help much on the *how* front.

One thing we do know: it wasn't some sort of divine dictation. God used the particular personalities, experiences, and situations of each of the writers to make their books unique. God guided each of them in such a way that each one revealed an important part about God's character and plans and about the way God works in the world.

So it's absolutely correct to think of the Bible as God's Word to us. Because, miraculously, it is.

Types and styles of writing

There are many different types of writing in the Bible. To impress an English teacher, you might call them *genres* of writing. For example—

History—where the deeds of kings and the political experiences of the nation of Israel are recorded.

Proverbs—where wise advice is stated in short, unforgettable, sometimes funny, sayings.

Poetry—almost everyone can quote at least a line or two from the poem-psalm that begins, "The Lord is my shepherd."

Biography—where the words and actions of Jesus are recorded by people who knew him face-to-face and heard his teaching with their own ears.

Songs—songs of love in the Song of Songs, which contains the unbeatable line, "Your teeth are white like newly sheared sheep just coming in from their bath"; and songs of praise to God, some of which we still sing today.

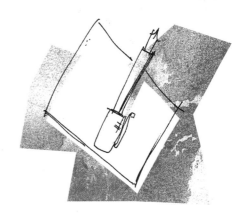

But is it true?

Imagine a tough New York cop interviewing witnesses to a bank robbery. If every witness walked into the office, sat down, and described what happened in exactly the same words as the others, the policeman would begin to suspect a conspiracy. It simply doesn't work that way. Honest witnesses will argue over the color of the getaway car, the height of the robber, and particularly the order in which things happened. After all, they are human beings, not video cameras. The police expect such differences. No criminal would ever be convicted if witnesses were considered unreliable because of different recollections of this sort.

It's precisely the same with the Bible. The very few and small disagreements over minor facts (opponents of the Bible love to point them out) just serve to prove the Bible isn't a hoax—it hasn't been carefully altered to make it look more reliable.

The big issues

Consider these issues: the origin of the universe, whether God exists, the problem of human good and evil, the question of what happens when we die…

If you were to discuss those issues in class, or even among friends, you could expect huge arguments. Billy thinks we've all descended from spacemen. Mary is convinced humans are basically good because her baby niece is so sweet. Alfred, the scientist, reckons we're just animals.

Yet all the authors of the Bible are in perfect agreement about these issues and many more equally complex ones. Add to this the fact that no archaeological dig ever discovered anything that disproves the history of the Bible, and you should begin to have more than enough evidence to conclude the Bible is true.

But there is more—changed lives

The best evidence that the Bible is truly God's book is its powerful effect on people's lives. Many, many people have been converted to Christianity simply by reading the Bible. It has the startling property of suddenly coming alive in the minds of people who read it and totally changing their lifelong thoughts and understanding about life.

It's because of this that there are millions of people on the planet who consider the Bible their most treasured possession. Risks are taken each day to smuggle Bibles into closed societies. The reason for the risk is that Christians living in those countries are so desperate for God's Word. No other book has quite that effect on people.

No other book is God's Word

Dancing
through the
Old Testament

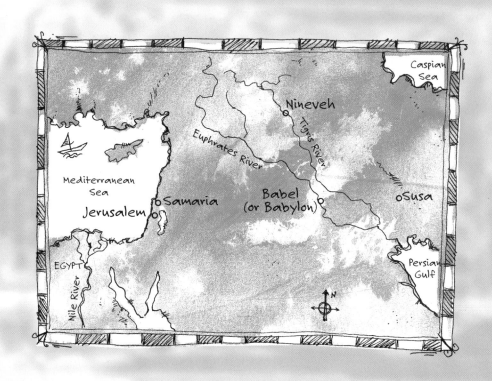

MAP OF THE ANCIENT NEAR EAST

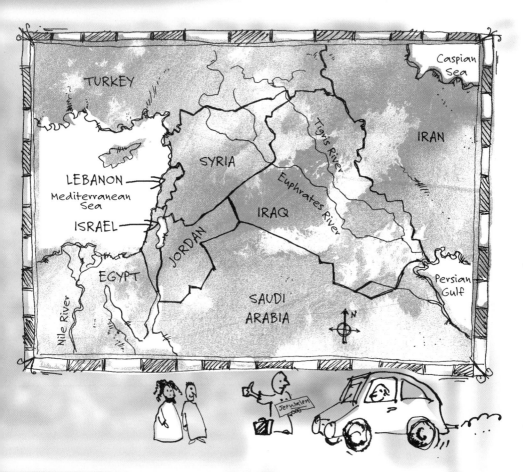

MAP OF THE MODERN NEAR EAST

Dancing through the Old Testament

Prehistory

The story so far...

There *is* no story so far!

"Dude. That is so totally cosmic!" Yes. Yes it is.

Maybe you'd rather be caught wearing a chest hair wig in public than risk using granola words like *cosmic*, but there's no better word to describe what happens in the first eleven chapters of Genesis.

Creation

Genesis starts with an awesome bang when God, just by speaking the words, creates the entire cosmos—time, space, stars, solar systems, planets. The whole universe and everything in it—including humans.

The fall

When Adam and Eve disobey God by munching on the one thing God left off the menu, the consequences are cosmic.

From now on there's a barrier between man and God, and the natural order of things will be for all men and women everywhere to disobey and displease, rather than obey and please, God.

Fortunately, God promised right there in the garden that one day he would make things right again. We call this **The Plan**.

The flood

This little episode could well have been the end of the human race if God hadn't taken a shine to one man, Noah. When God sent a flood of...wait for it...*cosmic* proportions to destroy humankind, he chose to save Noah and his family and start again with them.

He also saved a pair of each kind of animal, so Noah and his family would be able to have pets again after the flood. (The dinosaurs did have passages booked on the ark, but they had a slight disagreement with Noah about whether the cows were passengers or snacks, so Noah canceled their tickets.)

Nationalism

This section of the Bible finishes with the account of the division of the human race into separate nations with separate languages (which led to hundreds of ways to say "cosmic").

The Fathers of God's People

The story so far...

God made a beautiful, perfect world, which humans messed up so fast it wasn't funny. The human race was split into many separate groups. God formed **The Plan**, but making it happen required a special group of people to work with him. But who…?

Abraham

When NASA goes recruiting, they look for people made of *the right stuff*. God was looking for a man with just what it takes to follow him into uncharted territory. Abraham proved he had the right stuff when he heard God's voice and trusted him enough to do what he said.

A great nation

Later God said to Abraham, "I have a plan—I call it **The Plan**—that's going to be good news for people everywhere. Your children will become a great nation, and through them I'll carry out **The Plan**."

Cunning Plan

A son for Abraham

"Wow," said Abraham. "That sounds slick. But me and the missus don't have no kids, and we're well past our expiration date, if you know what I mean!"

They soon learned that when it comes to **The Plan**, nothing is too hard for God. It wasn't long before little Isaac was cooing and pooing like any other bouncing baby boy.

smelly baby

A grandson and great-grandsons

Isaac grew up, finished high school, went to college, landed a job, and settled down with a nice girl named Rebekah. They had twin sons named Esau and Jacob. Jacob was the one God chose to be the father of his special people.

One day God bumped into Jacob in the desert (God bumped into Jacob pretty hard, actually) and changed his name to Israel. Descendants of the shepherd formerly known as Jacob then became known as the children of Israel—or the Israelites.

27

The Israelites in Egypt

The story so far...

The world is a mess, but God has **The Plan** to make it right. He's chosen the man who will be the father of God's special accomplices in **The Plan**. The man's name is Israel, his children are the children of Israel, and his wife, of course, is Mrs. Israel.

Joseph (not Dennis Rodman)

Joseph

One of Jacob/Israel's sons was called Joseph (he would later become famous through a popular Andrew Lloyd Webber musical about his amazing technicolor dreamcoat). Joseph was a very talented young man, but so bigheaded he had to turn sideways to fit through doors. Joseph was his dad's favorite, which did nothing to endear Joseph to his many brothers.

(sorry this is in black & white)

I have a dream (so do we!)

Joseph had a dream from God that one day his whole family would bow down in front of him. He told his brothers all about it—funny, they didn't think it was as cool as Joseph did.

His brothers had a dream too—getting rid of Joseph. Killing him would give them the most pleasure, but selling him into slavery meant more money and less blood—proving blood is thicker than water, and cash is thicker than both.

Joseph in Egypt

In Egypt, Joseph's life was a roller coaster of pleasant and unpleasant experiences. God was with him, though, and in the end not only was he cured of his chronic big head, but he ended up as Pharaoh's right-hand man.

The family comes to stay

Do you remember **The Plan**? This is where it becomes obvious God was at work behind the scenes keeping his plan on track.

There was an incredible drought. We're not just talking about a ban on lawn-watering here—we're talking less moisture than a saltine in a clothes dryer. Soon the drought produced a famine. And wouldn't you know it? The only country in the world with anything like enough food was Joseph's new home, Egypt. People came from all over to beg, including Joseph's brothers.

While other people were turned away empty-handed and whole nations died out, the children of Israel were saved because Joseph forgave his brothers for their little slavery prank and invited everyone to come and live with him.

The Great Escape

The story so far...

The world is a mess, but God has **The Plan** to make it right. The children of Israel, his accomplices in **The Plan**, are now living in the great nation of Egypt.

Oy! We're not slaves—we're guests!

The Bible says that eventually a Pharaoh who didn't remember Joseph came to power.

Since the Nile region Yellow Pages didn't have a single building contractor, Pharaoh put the Israelites to work making bricks and building—pyramids, of course!

Would you stop that, please?

The Egyptians worked the Israelites hard and treated them cruelly, but no matter what happened, the Israelites multiplied like rabbits. In the end the Egyptians decided every Israelite baby boy must be thrown into the river as soon as he was born.

Moses

Sometimes you can bend the rules a little. One Israelite family threw their baby boy into the river all right, but they gave him his own little boat.

This little sea dog was called Moses, the person God was going to use to help his people escape from Egypt. The baby Moses was found river rafting by one of Pharaoh's daughters, who took him home and asked, "Can I keep him?" She raised Moses in the palace of Pharaoh.

Moses wondered what he could do to help his people. The answer was *not a lot*. When Moses killed an Egyptian, he fled the country, wearing dark glasses and a wig as he slipped through customs.

God takes over

Fortunately, Moses didn't have to do it on his own.

burning bush

29

God wanted his people out of Egypt, and he was happy to help things along.

When Moses returned to the Nile, God started sending plagues on Egypt. Before long, the authorities agreed it would be better for everyone concerned if the Israelites just left.

So they packed their bags and their animals and marched out of Egypt. Four hundred and some-odd years before, they had arrived as one small, starving family—they marched out as a whole nation.

The Wilderness

The story so far...

The world is a mess, but God has **The Plan** to make it right. The children of Israel are his chosen accomplices. Now they are out of Egypt and have become a mighty nation. But where will they live?

Introductions

God and the Israelites arranged to rendezvous at a spot in the desert called Mount Sinai. Moses spoke for the Israelites. God spoke for himself, setting down a few ground rules. Then it was full speed ahead for the land God promised Abraham that his children's children would live in.

A little bit lost

Sadly, things didn't quite go according to plan. It looked so simple on paper, but when push came to shove, the Israelites lacked faith in God and confidence in themselves. They were too scared of the big, ugly people already living in the land to go in and fight for it.

So instead they wandered for forty years in a small and barren wilderness, carrying God's tent around with them.

That's not the end of the story, though

God was not amused with their cowardice and grumbling, but he kept them alive, feeding them manna from heaven and making drinking fountains flow out of rocks when they were thirsty. He hadn't come this far in **The Plan** only to give up because of a yellow streak in some of the people he had chosen.

The Promised Land

The story so far...

The world is a mess, but God has **The Plan** to make things right. The children of Israel, his chosen accomplices, have wandered in a desert for forty years, but now the time has come to enter the Promised Land.

A new generation

God doesn't age at all, so he's quite willing to wait. Since one generation of Israelites were jelly-kneed cowards, he simply allowed the next generation to grow up. Forty years later this generation had had enough of living in tents in the wilderness, and they trusted God enough to be willing to fight for the Promised Land.

Joshua

The Israelites were led by an amazing man named Joshua. Joshua was Moses' right-hand man for many years and was well suited to the job at hand. He was part Clint Eastwood (action hero), part Nelson Mandela (intelligent and charismatic politician), and part Billy Graham (man of God).

After Moses' death, Joshua led the people across the Jordan River and into the Promised Land.

This town ain't big enough for the both of us!

God told his people it wasn't just a matter of moving in alongside the people already living in the Promised Land—they were to wipe them out completely.

This meant plenty of opportunities for Joshua to exercise his Clint Eastwood qualities as he led the children of Israel into battle after battle. When walls of great cities (like Jericho) fell down at a shout and the sun stood still in the sky, it became obvious God was stacking the deck in the Israelites' favor.

Oh, that's good enough, isn't it?

The Israelites soon got bored with all that fighting. What they really wanted was to settle down in a little bungalow with a nice view and enjoy the land full of milk and honey they had fought for.

Joshua put on his Nelson Mandela hat and carefully divided up the land, so each of the twelve tribes had its own patch to live in.

The Judges

The story so far . . .

The world is a mess, but God has **The Plan** to make things right again. The Israelites, the people God has chosen to be his accomplices in **The Plan,** are finally living in the Promised Land. But their laziness is about to cause them some problems.

What's his name again?

The Israelites were a forgetful bunch, and after only a few years of living in luxury in the Promised Land, they forgot all about God and all about **The Plan,** which was the reason they were there in the first place. All they wanted was to drink the milk and eat the honey that flowed in the land.

If that's the way you want it . . .

God decided to let the Israelites see how they liked life without him.

He allowed the people whom the Israelites had been too lazy to drive out of the land to attack and rob them. This got the Israelites' attention because suddenly life wasn't so luxurious anymore.

Someone else was drinking their milk and eating their honey.

The Israelites had a remarkable recovery of memory. Now they remembered it was God who gave them the land in the first place, and they called out to him to help them again: "Help! They've stolen our milk and honey!"

The judges

When the people cried out to him, God raised up a judge—a man or a woman with qualities similar to Joshua.

This judge would defeat the enemies, restore political order, and lead the people back to God. All in a day's work for a judge. Too bad they had to do it just about every day.

Over and over again

This occurred again and again and again, for about four hundred years!

The Kings of Israel

The story so far . . .

The world is a mess, but God has **The Plan** to make things right. The Israelites, God's chosen accomplices in **The Plan**, are in the Promised Land but going nowhere fast.

Down with the judges, up with the kings

Finally the Israelites had had it—right up to here—with the whole judges saga, and so for that matter had God.

God told Samuel, the last of the Judges, to anoint a young man named Saul to be the first king of Israel.

Saul

"Isn't he a good-looking guy? So tall and strong—I bet he could give those filthy Philistines a good thrashing. He's just the sort of man we want for king!"

Saul looked the part, but he turned out not to be quite the man God wanted.

David

When Saul offended God one time too many, Samuel anointed a new king named David.

Saul didn't particularly like the idea of David becoming king, as he was rather partial to the job himself—especially the perks, like his flashy, high-powered, government-maintained chariot. Talk about horse power!

So Saul chased David all over the country. He should have known it's never a good idea to get in God's way when he's working on **The Plan**.

A clue, a clue!

The next piece of **The Plan** came to light when Saul died and David became king.

God told David that, from his descendants, would come one whom God would call his Son and who would reign as king forever and forever. Now, who might that be?

Solomon

When David died, his wise son Solomon became king of Israel.

On Solomon's watch, the nation of Israel became fabulously wealthy and was known through all the earth as a splendid resort destination.

Things had never looked better as far as **The Plan** was concerned, but they didn't stay that way for long.

Civil War and a Divided Nation

The story so far . . .

The world is a mess, but God has **The Plan** to make everything right again. The Israelites, God's chosen accomplices, are living in the Promised Land and prospering under wise king Solomon.

Bigger and badder than ever before

Oh no! Just when things were going so well!

When Solomon died, his son, Rehoboam, became king. The new king suffered a bit of a hot flush when the power went to his head. All of a sudden he's coming off all big and macho, trying to beat his people into submission.

Well, we'll play on our own then!

This bit of carefully considered politics didn't have quite the effect Rehoboam had hoped. Instead of scaring the people into obedience, it made them angry. They decided to start their own country without him.

"We don't need you, you big bully," they cried, and they stormed off to their own homes in the northern part of the Promised Land. They made a much nicer man, called Jeroboam, their king.

Two nations, two kings, two altars

From this time on, God's special people, the Israelites, were split into two nations with two of everything. One king ruled the northern kingdom, and one ruled the southern kingdom.

The people of the northern kingdom worshiped God in a city named Bethel, and the people of the southern kingdom continued worshiping at the temple in Jerusalem.

Use these clips to hold pairs of socks together

IQ 230

The Destruction of the Northern Kingdom

The story so far...

The world is a mess, but God has **The Plan** to make things right. His chosen accomplices, the Israelites, have now split into two distinct nations—the northern and the southern kingdoms.

Here we go! Here we go! Here we go!

Now that they were on their own with their own nation and their own king, the people of the northern kingdom set about irritating God as much as possible.

In fairness, this probably wasn't their actual plan, but they couldn't have done a better job if they'd tried.

Watch it!

God wasn't slow in telling them they were way out of line. He warned them to straighten up and fly right—or get ready for a nasty crash.

But the people were enjoying themselves too much to worry about moaning old prophets, and they carried on as if they didn't have a care in the world.

Somewhere to the north...

The people failed to notice the growth of a nation called Assyria to the north of them. The Assyrians were strong and powerful people who were beginning to look with greedy eyes toward their wealthy neighbors.

God had promised he would judge the northern kingdom, and the Assyrians were just the people for the job.

Destruction

Little did the people of the northern kingdom realize their whole nation was about to become like a banana under a steamroller.

Before they really knew what was happening, the king of Assyria swept down from the north, defeated all their armies, destroyed their towns, and carried the people away into captivity.

The northern kingdom was no more. R.I.P.

— wise Solomon

The Destruction of the Southern Kingdom

The story so far...

God's world is a mess, but he has **The Plan** to make things right. The Israelites, his chosen accomplices, are split into two distinct kingdoms. The northern kingdom has just been squashed lifeless by the Assyrians. What will happen to the southern kingdom?

Down south

The kings and people of the southern kingdom were better at following God than the people of the northern kingdom. But not by much.

"Better, but still not good enough," said the prophets. God sent the prophets to warn them they too were cruisin' for a bruisin'. "You've got to learn to follow God all the time, and not just when it suits you," said the stern prophets.

We are the champions!

After he destroyed the northern kingdom, the king of Assyria set his sights on the southern kingdom as a little two-for-one bonus.

Things did not look good for the southern kingdom, but the king of Assyria was about to learn, like others before him, that God was in control and only *he* says what should happen and when. In the middle of the night, an angel from God went out into the middle of the Assyrian army and slaughtered thousands of the soldiers.

While the king of Assyria was walking around the next morning, knee-deep in dead bodies, he had a blinding flash of inspiration.

"Something fishy's going on here," he said, and hightailed it out of Jerusalem.

We are invincible

For a while, this little episode had a good effect on the people of the southern kingdom—they remembered who God was.

But soon they were convinced they were invincible. They thought God loved them too much to let anything bad happen to them, and they could do whatever they wanted without fear.

Wrong!

The Babylonians

Somewhere to the north, the bully-boy Assyrians were being soundly thrashed by the *mucho mas macho* Babylonians. Soon the Babylonians were looking with greedy eyes toward the little nation of Israel in the south.

One hundred years after the northern kingdom bit the dust, the southern kingdom was wiped out by the Babylonians, and the people were carried away into captivity. And that was that.

"What happened to **The Plan**, we ask ourselves."

The Return from Captivity

The story so far...

The world is a mess, but God has **The Plan** to make things right. Unfortunately his accomplices, the Israelites, are all living in captivity in the cruel empires of the north. Is it all over? Is **The Plan** dead in the water?

Don't panic!

As the people of the southern kingdom were being led into captivity by the Babylonians, things looked pretty darn grim.

There was one voice of hope. The prophet Jeremiah prophesied that, though deliverance wasn't exactly right around the corner, the captivity would end after 70 years, and then the people would be allowed to go home. It might not have helped the older ones much, but Jeremiah knew that, in God's hand, **The Plan** was still alive.

New management

Now that the Babylonians had served their purpose in **The Plan**, God was about to judge them for their cruelty. He raised up a new empire ruled by kinder, gentler warriors. They weren't as cruel as the Babylonians, but they were still formidable soldiers, and they kicked some serious Babylonian booty.

Once they were in charge, they allowed captive peoples to return to their own lands to rebuild their cities and nations. Some of the people of the southern kingdom accepted the opportunity to return to Israel to rebuild the cities and, particularly, the very holy temple of God.

Oh, now we get it!

Once back in the Promised Land God gave them, the Israelites were determined never to be moved out of it again, not by anyone. They had been cured of their tendency to forget God and worship other idols by their horrible experiences of destruction and captivity.

They were by no means perfect, but they finally realized what made them unique and special was their relationship to the one true God. Finally, they wanted to play their part in implementing **The Plan**.

What this all led to . . .

For four hundred years after the people of the southern kingdom returned to their homes, all was quiet as far as **The Plan** was concerned.

Then, one winter's night, some shepherds washing their socks . . . I mean, watching the box . . . I mean, watching their flocks, were treated to an impromptu concert.

"No," they were told by the lead singer. "We're not rehearsing for the Miss Palestine Pageant, and we're definitely not wearing bathing suits under our evening wear. We're angels! We've come to celebrate the birth of a very special child."

Having been told by the angels that the baby was to be found in a local farmyard, the shepherds set off to find him.

"Perhaps they're hiding in a farmyard to avoid the paparazzi," said one shepherd.

When they arrived, they found the little guy in his mother's arms.

This newborn boy, delivered in a farmyard in an obscure village in Israel, was the end result of **The Plan** worked out by God over hundreds of years with the children of Israel as his accomplices.

The boy, though poor, was an Israelite—of the nation God had miraculously delivered from Egypt and made his own.

He was of the southern kingdom—whose people God had brought back from terrible exile to live once more in the Promised Land.

He was a descendant of David—the king to whom God had promised a great-great-great-grandson who would rule forever.

This little baby was the only Son of God, the

Savior of the world. Already, by dying and rising again, he has started to clean up the mess the world is in and make things right again. He will finish the job one day when he returns as Lord of all creation to rule in peace forever.

There's lots more information on this incredible person in the New Testament part of your Bible.

Don't you just love it when a plan comes together!

shepherd awakened

The Five Books

THE OLD

Genesis Exodus
Leviticus Numbers
Deuteronomy

Joshua Judges **Ruth**
1 Samuel 2 Samuel 1 Kings 2
Kings **1 Chronicles**
2 Chronicles Ezra Nehemiah
Esther

The Historical Books

ALL ACCESS

BACKSTAGE PASS · ADMIT 1

Backstage Pass

Genesis
Exodus
Leviticus
Numbers
Deuteronomy

The Books of Poetry and Wisdom

TESTAMENT

Job **Psalms** Proverbs
Ecclesiastes Song
of Songs

Isaiah **Jeremiah**
Lamentations Ezekiel
Daniel Hosea Joel Amos Obadiah
Jonah Micah Nahum Habakkuk
Zephaniah Haggai Zechariah
Malachi

The Old Testament Prophets

The Five Books

Are they worth reading?

Appearing to be rich was a huge misfortune at my school, and there was only one person in my class who had the misfortune to seem to be well-off. So we made him pay for it. I guess we were reverse snobs. He also had a rather large nose—which didn't help any. Based on those two impressions, this kid was known as the big-nosed snob. How's that for wit, hey?

Years later—eleventh grade to be exact—he became my friend. Not because I was feeling sorry for him, but because he turned out to be a really nice guy. He certainly wasn't a snob, and a big nose is a very minor disability unless the nostrils point upward in which case there's a drowning hazard.

First impressions, especially impressions borrowed from others, are not renowned for their accuracy. All that's to say: don't listen to other people's impressions of the first five books of the Bible. Read them yourself—they're well worth it.

But aren't they boring and irrelevant?

"Pages and pages of mind-numbingly tedious laws about not eating pork. Chapter after chapter of instructions about the number of tassels per foot on the curtains in the tabernacle. Jesus did away with all that Old Testament stuff. Why would I waste valuable time reading that when I could be doing something worth while—like watching championship wrestling on cable."

Wrong, so wrong. Typical misconceptions, sure, but still wrong. If we make the effort and go about it the right way, the first five books of the Bible are incredibly interesting and exciting to read.

Why are they grouped together?

The Law and the Profits—sounds like the title of a Learning Channel documentary about police corruption, doesn't it? Actually, it's what Jewish people called their Scripture. That's *prophets,* not *profits.*

The first five books are what Jewish people call the Law. They are also known as the Five Fifths of Moses, which means they only make complete sense and tell the whole story when taken together. That title gives us a hint as to who the Jews think wrote them—the greatest prophet and leader of the whole Old Testament, the adopted son of Pharaoh of Egypt and God's chosen deliverer for his people—Moses himself.

The five books cover a period of time that is, at the very least, as long as the rest of the Bible put together—from the creation of the world to the coming of the children of Israel to the Promised Land and Moses' death. (It makes sense he would have to stop writing then, doesn't it?)

All of Jewish religion and identity is based upon these books, and they couldn't rate them more highly if they tried.

Do they have an overall theme?

It might not be right at the top of your to-do list yet, but finding someone you want to marry and then persuading the person that you're the one to marry is no easy task. I won't tell you which part gave me the most trouble.

The main theme of the first five books is God's choosing of Israel to be his special people (not unlike a marriage relationship) and the way he wins her.

Once they get together, after some very exciting adventures, they have to decide on the rules for living happily ever after.

So what does this have to do with me?

The New Testament makes it clear that we as Christians are now part of God's chosen people, like the Israelites in the Old Testament. As we read the first five books, we can learn a lot about how God wants us to live, and we can be reassured he loves us and has chosen us to be his own.

By reading these books, we can understand who we are and what our purpose and place in the world is.

eye movement

finger movement

XTRA LARGE CHIPS

TV remote

The Book of Genesis

A book with answers for those who wonder about life's big questions

First off . . .

There was a time when films about people suffering from amnesia were popular. But imagine how scary it would be: you wake up in a hospital bed (not a pleasant experience anyway) and don't know who you are.

Now I know that in real life, Aunt Daisy, who'd been sitting by your bed for hours eating all the chocolates, would screech with excitement and be very quick to tell you all about yourself and your wonderful family. But what if she didn't?

As a human race we do suffer from a kind of amnesia. You can't even remember your own birth—can you?—let alone the birth of humankind. The book of Genesis is given to us by God to perform the Aunt Daisy role, to remind us of who we are, where we come from, what our purpose is, and what's good and bad.

Ground covered

apple

There are strains of thought that will eat your mind alive. For example: "Does she like me?" No matter how much time and brain power you put into that question, no matter how many times you go over the evidence—"he burped when he walked past me in the corridor so he must like me," or "she didn't laugh when I burped in the corridor so she must hate me"—you never come up with an actual answer. Your brain just gets hung up in a never-ending loop until it jams like an old school computer you can't shut down.

Genesis tackles questions like that, and as old as it is, it offers answers that are still as believable as anything else in the marketplace of ideas. Genesis is particularly about beginnings, which is what *genesis* means: the beginnings of the universe; the beginnings of humankind; the beginnings of God's chosen people; the beginnings of God's relationship with his creation.

Main themes

The book of Genesis can be split into two parts, both dealing with beginnings.

The first eleven chapters

These first chapters deal with the beginnings of the whole universe and of humankind in particular.

In the form of epic stories, Genesis traces the history of humanity and explains such diverse issues as how sin entered the world, why there are different languages and nations, and how God deals with us when we sin.

Chapters 12-50

Now that the minor matter of the beginning of the universe is out of the way—that didn't take long—we can proceed to the matter of the beginnings of God's chosen people and his plans for them.

We start with a man named Abraham (originally Abram) and finish with his great-grandson Joseph.

But what about me?

Genesis hits on many of the big philosophical questions non-Christians ask.

Q. Where do we come from?

Q. Why are we here?

Q. Why are there so much evil and suffering in the world?

Central characters

Adam and Eve—read Genesis chapters 1–4

Noah and his ark—read Genesis 5:28–9:29

Abraham—read Genesis 11:27–25:11

Joseph—read Genesis 37:1–50:26

interesting bits

Creation—read Genesis 1:1–2:25

The Flood—read Genesis 6:1–8:22

The Tower of Babel—read Genesis 11:1–9

Sodom and Gomorrah—read Genesis 18:16–19:29

looks like rain

two-headed sneeds think the weather will blow over

GENESIS

The Book of

Exodus

A story for adventure lovers that shows God's power and faithfulness

First off . . .

What sort of films do you like watching? If you like nice, gentle romantic films, this might not be the book for you. If, on the other hand, you like your films fast-moving and full of action and special effects, read on.

Ground covered

Exodus tells what may be the most exciting story in the Bible: the story of how God delivered his people from their slavery in Egypt and made an agreement with them to be their God forever.

Main themes

Exodus can be split into two parts, an adventure and a marriage of sorts.

Escape from Egypt

It would take filmmakers with the skills and budgets of Spielberg, Lucas, and Cameron to do justice to this part of the book as a live-action film. A bush that's on fire but doesn't burn might not be too taxing for them, but that's only the beginning. From there on things get a little unusual.

Walking sticks turn into snakes and back again. Rivers run with blood. Zillions of frogs and locusts swarm through the land of Egypt. Every first-born human and animal in Egypt dies at the same time. And in a great finale, the whole Israelite nation passes through the middle of the sea just before the waves come crashing back down on all the pursuing armies of Egypt. I'm ready for my close-up, Mr. DeMille.

But what about me?

As we read this section of Exodus, we see not only the power of God, but also his love for his people. That's a comforting combination when we remember Christians are now among his chosen people.

"Me Tarzan, you Jane" or "Me God, you my people"

Boys often fantasize about what impressive feats they could perform to impress the girls they like. In a daydream, fighting off ten gangsters and then carrying a girl away in your arms seems entirely reasonable. A fist here, a boot there, a finger poked just so. But of course things never quite turn out that way.

For God, though, it had worked. He'd really pulled off helping Israel escape from Egypt. And now that he'd saved them and gotten their attention, it was time for a marriage ceremony if they were going to live happily ever after.

The second part of the book of Exodus is, in effect, the marriage ceremony of the Old Testament. The wedding took place about three months after Israel left Egypt, at the foot of a mountain called Sinai. God appeared to the nation of Israel and through Moses made his promises to them. In return they agreed to keep all his laws.

Starting a pattern that runs all through the Old Testament, the Israelites almost immediately committed adultery by worshiping another god in the form of a golden calf. Fortunately for them, and for all of us today, God is more faithful in his promises than we are, and he took them back and continued to love them. Try to remember that the next time you feel you've let God down.

interesting bits

Moses' early life—read Exodus 2:1–4:31

The escape from Egypt—read Exodus 7:1–14:31

Food and drink from God—read Exodus 16:1–17:7

God on Mount Sinai—read Exodus 19:1–25

The Ten Commandments—read Exodus 20:1–17

The golden calf—read Exodus 32:1–35

EXODUS

The Book of
Leviticus

How to live with God without getting struck by lightning

First off . . .

The police—do you love them or hate them? It tends to depend on the situation, doesn't it?

If you were running full-tilt boogey from gangsters, that blue uniform would be the most welcome sight in the world. On the other hand, if you were enjoying a bit of winter fun launching snowballs at passing cars, the appearance of that same blue uniform could make you feel physically sick.

That just about sums up our love-hate attitude about rules and laws. We love them when they're working for us but hate them when they restrict us.

Ground covered

Leviticus covers the laws God gave to the ancient Israelites. The laws cover everything from food to sexuality, and from blood sacrifices to baldness. There are religious laws, laws that focus on cleanness in food preparation or the quarantine of sick people, and others that deal with how to treat the poor and people who work for you.

But what about me?

There's nothing more infuriating than living, even for a short space of time, with someone who's completely your opposite. She stays up late; you like to get up early. You like your room to have a lived-in feel; he goes crazy if a piece of clothing so much as hits the floor.

In those situations, sometimes the only way to avoid bloodshed is to create rules for living together, like the ones God gave the Israelites. Fortunately for us, what Jesus did means we can now approach God without having to slaughter cute little animals!

interesting bits

How some offerings are to be made—read Leviticus 1:1–17

The first priests are appointed—read Leviticus 8:1–36

Charming rules about skin disease for acne sufferers—read Leviticus 13:1–46

Bank holidays for God's people—read Leviticus 23:1–44

Rewards and punishments—read Leviticus 26:1–39

The Book of
Numbers

A book for those who are inclined to moan

First off . . .

The Israelites were the biggest bunch of moaners in history. God kept them going round and round in circles till they learned to shut their mouths and trust him.

Ground covered

Numbers picks up the story where Exodus left off. It's the sad story of Israel's 40 years of wandering in the wilderness.

So, why were they there for so long? It wasn't plan A, that's for certain. Plan A was that they go in immediately and conquer the land God promised them. But they were scared of fighting and rebellious against Moses their leader.

God took both of these things personally, so he made plan B: wander in the desert for 40 years till all the cowardly rebellious people die off, then God will take a new generation into the Promised Land.

But what about me?

Some people give up too easily. Some friends will blow off a football game just because it's raining. Others will refuse to leave the house because their hair is not quite right.

Fortunately for us, God never gives up. We might blow it in a big way and think we've messed up our lives forever, but as the story told in Numbers shows, God can always get us back on course.

interesting bits

The people start moaning—read Numbers 11:1–12:16

The spies go out spying—read Numbers 13:1–33

The ground opens up—read Numbers 16:1–40

Even Moses blows it—read Numbers 20:1–13

Balaam and the talking donkey—read Numbers 22:1–24:25

A new leader is appointed—read Numbers 27:12–23

The Book of
Deuteronomy

A book for those who wonder why God gives us rules

First off . . .

I know this is a disgusting thought, but have you ever considered that some of the music you listen to on the radio and some of the albums you buy might be by exactly the same bands and singers your parents liked when they were teenagers?

What could be more uncool than buying a CD, then coming back home to find your dad's got the same album on one of those old vinyl records? And not just the Beatles but the Rolling Stones, Jimmy Buffet, the Eagles, Eric Clapton.

The book of Deuteronomy is Moses' farewell gig. This is where he gives some of the big-hit sermon-messages from God again, this time to a whole new generation.

Ground covered

Deuteronomy is the record of a number of sermons Moses preached to the Israelites just before he died and before they entered the Promised Land. In his talks he covered all God had spoken to him at Mount Sinai and the following years.

The messages needed to be given again because the people entering the Promised Land were a completely new generation from their parents and grandparents who were saved from Egypt.

Main theme

Some of the best teachers initially appear to be the most harsh, unkind, and strict. For the first few weeks of school, you live in fear and tell everyone you've never had a worse teacher. But once they've established discipline in the classroom, they gradually relax, and you find they're human after all (contrary to what you may have heard, all teachers are human). The things that were hard at first make the class enjoyable in the end.

God sometimes appeared to the Israelites as hard and scary. He thundered on Mount Sinai, he set very high standards for the people to keep, and he killed those who rebelled against him.

In Deuteronomy, Moses emphasizes that God's love for the people is behind all his laws. God chose them to be his people not because they deserved it, but because he loved them. The laws were intended to make them happy and healthy. The consequences for disobeying God's laws were the natural and supernatural outcomes of disobedience. The consequences were *never* about God hating his people.

But what about me?

It's easy to focus on the *don'ts* of Christianity. Sometimes it seems like all the fun things our friends do are off limits for us.

Deuteronomy teaches an important lesson. God is not a killjoy or an out-of-touch geezer who doesn't understand what life is like for young people today. He's our perfectly loving and perfectly wise heavenly Father whose laws can keep us safe and happy.

interesting bits

Love God and He will help you—read Deuteronomy 6:1–25

God chose you because he loves you—read Deuteronomy 7:7–16

How to treat neighbours who are poor—read Deuteronomy 15:7–11

The results of obeying or disobeying—read Deuteronomy 28:1–68

The death of Moses—read Deuteronomy 32:48–52, 34:1–12

DEUTERONOMY

Mick and Keith at the Home for British Invasion Veterans.

The Five Books

Genesis Exodus
Leviticus Numbers
Deuteronomy

Joshua Judges **Ruth**
1 Samuel 2 Samuel 1 Kings 2
Kings **1 Chronicles**.
2 Chronicles Ezra Nehemiah
Esther

The Historical Books

The Books of Poetry and Wisdom

Backstage Pass

Joshua
Judges
Ruth
1 Samuel
2 Samuel
1 Kings
2 Kings
1 Chronicles
2 Chronicles
Ezra
Nehemiah
Esther

TESTAMENT

Job **Psalms** Proverbs
Ecclesiastes Song
of Songs

Isaiah **Jeremiah**
Lamentations Ezekiel
Daniel Hosea Joel Amos Obadiah
Jonah Micah Nahum Habakkuk
Zephaniah Haggai Zechariah
Malachi

The Old Testament Prophets

53

The Historical Books

What are they?

Do you prefer cross-country or track running? Neither? Personally, I'd choose a run through the park any day of the week. I'm afraid I get bored going round and round in circles. Running is hard enough work as it is. I need at least to feel I'm getting somewhere.

Most of the other religions of the world view history as cyclical—like going round and round a track without ever actually getting anywhere. But as Christians we believe history is linear—it's progressing toward a fixed point. God has a purpose and a plan he's working out in the world, and one day time will end and a new heaven and a new earth will begin.

This group of Old Testament books tells the history of the nation of Israel from the time they first entered the Promised Land through their return from captivity, which is where the Old Testament finishes.

So why did God bother to include history books in the Bible?

Do you know what an *oxymoron* is? No, it's not a treatment for zits, and it has nothing to do with someone who's intellectually challenged. An oxymoron is a phrase that at first seems to be contradictory—like thunderous silence, bitter sweet, or short sermon.

The books we're looking at are sometimes called *prophetic history,* which may seem like an oxymoron—isn't prophecy about the future and history about the past?

What prophetic history really means is these books were written not just as records of the past, but to show what God was doing and what his purpose was in all of the events that are recorded. Right from the moment they were written, these books were intended to teach us about God.

So they're not real history then?

Some people think because the purpose of the books was to teach people about God, they can't be trusted to be true like *real* history books.

Scattered throughout these books are sources of information the writers used to make sure what they wrote was accurate. These sources included court records from the times of the kings, biographies about the great men and women (like

interesting bits

Undercover spying mission—read Joshua 2:1–24

The famous battle of Jericho—read Joshua 6:1–27

The sun stands still—read Joshua 10:1–14

Joshua's final words of challenge—read Joshua 23:1–24:27

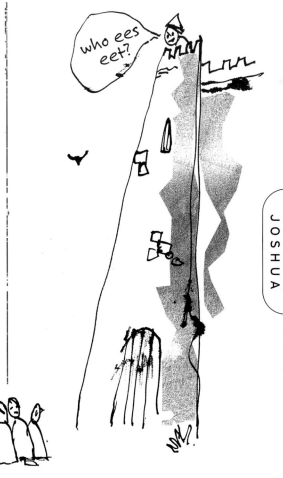

JOSHUA

The Book of
Judges

A book for those of us who make the same mistakes again and again

First off . . .

Vicious circles are not related to slime or swamp men or any of the other evil, flesh-eating characters from Hollywood's B movies. They are bad patterns that keep repeating themselves, like the vicious circle the Israelites find themselves trapped in here.

Ground covered

In my humble opinion, weekdays are nothing more than bridges between weekends—when life is really lived.

The book of Judges bridges the time between Israel's conquering the land and crowning a king. Their vicious circle was forgetting God...getting into trouble...screaming to God for help...God anointing a judge to save his people...times of peace...forgetting God...getting into trouble...and so on.

Main theme

Who do you think would still love you if you made the same stupid mistake for the billionth time? Possibly only your mother!

God shows his incredible patience with his people in the book of Judges. He saves them from their own stupidity time and time again.

But what about me?

We can all see ourselves in the pattern above. In good times we forget God and go off to do our own thing. In rough times we remember him and ask for help. Then we forget about him again.

God is so patient with us. We must never be afraid to go to him for help, but if we can break out of the vicious cycle, we'll be much better off.

Central characters

These judges didn't wear white wigs and hand down criminal sentences. They were warriors whom God anointed to unite the Israelites and defeat their enemies.

interesting bits

The first Judge sets the pattern—read Judges 3:7–11

Deborah the woman Judge—read Judges chapters 4–5

Gideon the coward becomes Judge Dredd—read chapters Judges 6–8

Samson the Judge—read Judges chapters 13–16

The Book of Ruth

A book for those who like a good romance

A book of love, loyalty, and redemption. Ruth is a love story from the time of the judges. About time too after all the war and battle that have been going on recently!

Read it—it's only four chapters long.

Ruth

Her man
Boaz

The Books of
1 Samuel &
2 Samuel

Books for those who <u>think</u> they know what they want

First off . . .

"We don't have anyone to put on the front of *Hello* magazine," they cried. "We need a royal family!"

In the time of 1 and 2 Samuel, the cry from the people was for a king.

Ground covered

The two books cover the reigns of Israel's first two kings, both of whom were appointed by God through Samuel, the last of the judges.

The first, Saul, showed all that could be wrong with a king. The second, David, made many mistakes, but he was Israel's greatest ruler. (He must be impressive—Richard Gere played him in a film.)

Main theme

God knew a king was not what Israel needed, but the plan might work if the king served under God's ultimate rule, as God's chosen leader.

In the first part of David's reign, the country enjoyed incredible success in war and every other way because he served God. However, when the king went wrong and sinned and rebelled, it affected the whole of the nation.

But what about me?

Here's a little brainteaser for you. Would you rather God give you what you want or what you need?

Sometimes God gives us what we ask for and not what he knows we need (like giving the Israelites a king). At these times we often start off happy and end up sad (the Israelites soon came to resent their kings). Other times, God refuses what we ask for but gives us what he knows we need. These times are better—we may start sad, but we finish happy because God knows best.

big bloke

Central characters

Samuel, last judge and kingmaker—early life—read 1 Samuel 1:1–3:21, then through the rest of 1 Samuel

Saul, first king of Israel, becomes king—read 1 Samuel 9:1–10:27

David, great king of Israel (see Interesting bits)

interesting bits

The people demand a king—read 1 Samuel 8:1–22

David fights the giant—read 1 Samuel 17:1–58

David and Jonathan—read 1 Samuel 18:1–20:42

David becomes king of all Israel—read 2 Samuel 5:1–5

God's promise to David—read 2 Samuel 7:1–17

David and Bathsheba—read 2 Samuel 11:1–12:25

bop!

large sword

COME ON HAVE A GO IF U FINK YOR HARD ENUFF

little stone

small guy

The Books of
1 Kings and 2 Kings

Books for those who are willing to swim against the current

First off . . .

Few things in life are as fun as riding a bike downhill fast. The wind rushes past, there's no effort, and the danger gets the adrenaline pumping.

1 and 2 Kings see Israel rushing faster and faster downhill on a bike without brakes. It's just a matter of time before they crash and burn.

Ground covered

and I also have good teeth-brush twice a day, I always say

Solomon

1 and 2 Kings cover about 400 years of Israel's history, all of it downhill. From the peak of David and Solomon's reign, past the sad split into the two separate nations of Israel and Judah, and then down to the bottom of the hill and a big and painful crash.

Within 150 years of each other, both of the nations were conquered and the survivors carried off into captivity.

Main theme

Only a stupid teacher would hand out detentions without explaining what they're for. If you don't understand why you're being punished, you can't learn.

1 and 2 Kings were probably compiled from earlier accounts while the people were in exile—God's punishment for their sin. The books showed God hadn't let the people down—the people walked away from God. The hope of the writers swas that if everyone understood this, they wouldn't make the same mistakes next time.

But what about me?

As you read 1 and 2 Kings, look for the outstanding kings and prophets who were prepared to go against the flow and stand for God in their day. God is still looking for people with the guts to take a stand for him and not just take the easy options.

Central characters

Solomon, the richest king—read 1 Kings 1:28–11:43

Ahab and his wife Jezebel, the worst of the worst, and the pattern for all the bad kings who followed—read 1 Kings 16:29–22:40

Elijah and Elisha, two great prophets who followed God even when all the others were doing their own thing—read 1 Kings 17:1–21:29, 2 Kings 1:1–13:21

you wait for ages for a chariot

chariot

woosh

Elisha

fire

Elijah

priests of Baal, no fire

interesting bits

Solomon's wisdom—read 1 Kings 3:1–28, 4:29–34

The nation is split—read 1 Kings 12:1–33

Joash the youngest king—read 2 Kings 11:1–12:21

Josiah, at last a good king—read 2 Kings 22:1–23:30

The northern kingdom destroyed—read 2 Kings 17:1–18

Judah is also destroyed—read 2 Kings 25:1–21

1 KINGS / 2 KINGS

The Books of
1 Chronicles &
2 Chronicles

Books for people who never give up

you're right—
you did leave
the gas on

First off . . .

I've yet to hear a real die-hard football fan complain about seeing replays of a great touchdown from seven different angles. That's because each camera angle shows you something different about the player's skills.

Lots of people do complain that 1 and 2 Chronicles are just a replay of Kings. Well, they are, but from a different camera angle, so we learn a lot more about what was going on.

Ground covered

Historically, the Chronicles cover the same period as 1 and 2 Kings, but they focus on different things.

- ▸ Good times instead of bad times
- ▸ Kings descended from David instead of all the kings
- ▸ The southern kingdom of Judah instead of both kingdoms
- ▸ The temple and worship, instead of false gods and idolatry

Main theme

Eventually some people from the nation of Judah returned home from their long captivity. As they tried to rebuild their homes and their nation, it was important that they know why they failed in the past and be encouraged about the future.

The most important lesson for them to learn was that the success of their nation depended absolutely on the way the people related to God. When they followed him, things went well. When they left him behind or worshiped other gods, things went downhill fast.

But what about me?

A writer named G. K. Chesterton, who constantly struggled to be on time, once said the only way to catch a train is to miss the one before it. Others have said you've only really failed once you've given up trying.

Failures are okay provided you get up and try again. That's a great attitude to have in our lives, especially in our relationship with God.

...and here's the tag at second base from our mini cam on the international space station

interesting bits

The first people to return—read 1 Chronicles 9:1–34

David's mighty army—read 1 Chronicles chapters 11–12

David's prayer for the temple—read 1 Chronicles 29:10–20

God comes to the temple—read 2 Chronicles 7:1–22

God defends Jerusalem—read 2 Chronicles 32:1–23

The Book of

 Ezra

A book about balance

First off . . .

Did you ever watch the old Disney film *Swiss Family Robinson*? The family shipwrecked on a desert island and had to learn to survive without the conveniences of home, as well as fight off all sorts of enemies.

That's not unlike the Jews in the book of Ezra returning to a destroyed city.

let's play hide and seek

Ground covered

Ezra tells the story of the Jews who were allowed to return home to Jerusalem after their time in captivity. They had to learn to survive, not only physically but also spiritually.

Main theme

Here's an easy question: If you add dirty water to clean water, is the bucket full of clean or dirty water?

Ezra knew it would be the same with the Jews returning to Jerusalem. If they mixed with the evil, ungodly people living around Jerusalem, they would end up dirty too. So he commanded the people to keep God's laws, confess their sin, and not mix with the surrounding people.

But what about me?

I have always wanted to try tightrope walking—though preferably a few feet, rather than a few hundred feet, off the ground.

As Christians, we're called to walk a sort of tightrope. Since we have God's Spirit to empower us, we don't have to steer as far clear of nonbelievers as the Jews had to. But we're called to find the right balance of being *in* the world, among non-Christians, but not *of* the world (with them but not quite like them).

That's a balancing act to work on for the rest of our lives.

Central characters

Cyrus, Xerxes, and Artaxerxes were all rulers in the lands to which the Israelites had been taken captive—read Ezra chapters 1–6

Ezra was a great scholar and teacher, and a direct descendant of the high priests in the time of the kings—read Ezra chapters 7–10

oooh

aahh

EZRA

67

The Book of
Nehemiah

A book that proves it's possible to win against the odds—especially if you've got God on your side!

First off . . .

In ancient times, a city without walls was about as useful as an armored car with a convertible top.

Unwalled cities were vulnerable to neighboring tribes who would simply march right in and head right off with people's TVs, VCRs, PCs, and lots of other good stuff. Nehemiah is all about the rebuilding of Jerusalem's walls.

Ground covered

One day you might have to choose between a job where you'll get paid lots of money and one you believe is important.

Nehemiah had a safe and probably well-paid job, serving the king of Persia. When he heard that those who returned to Jerusalem had not yet rebuilt the walls of the city, he knew he was the man to do the job, but it would mean giving up a lot.

Main theme

A friend of mine called Greenie (nothing at all to do with his nostrils) was the fullback on our football team. The problem was he was short, skinny, and desperately trying to catch up physically. He was also totally fearless. Overconfident players would run straight at Greenie, certain they could avoid a tackle—only to be flattened by the little guy.

As humans, we love the underdog, the person who beats all the odds. In Nehemiah we watch the Jews, with God's help, beat all the odds.

But what about me?

Nehemiah never gave up. There were times when he was being threatened, and his nice safe job serving the king must have seemed like a dream—but he kept going.

Persistence is a trait God seems to appreciate and work with. Next time you hit a wall, keep going, keep pushing, and let God help you through.

interesting bits

Nehemiah decides to go to Jerusalem— read Nehemiah 1:1–2:10

Keeping on in spite of threats—read Nehemiah 4:1–23

The people hear a sermon from Ezra—read Nehemiah 8:1–18

Celebrations for the completed walls—read Nehemiah 12:27–43

The Book of

Esther

A book for those who like their heroes to be women

First off . . .

Do you prefer your heroines to be all-action types, like Princess Leia in *Star Wars* and Ripley in the *Alien* films or the more traditional feminine type? Esther splits the difference. Although Esther is very beautiful and she never shoots anyone, this is no love story. Esther ends up saving the whole nation of Israel through her bravery.

Ground covered

The story told in Esther takes place at the same time as the events in the books of Ezra and Nehemiah. It's the story of a beautiful young Jewish girl who is chosen to be one of the queens of the Persian king Xerxes.

While she is queen, a plot is hatched to destroy all of the Jewish people. Fortunately for them, Esther is in the right place at the right time to stop the evil plan.

It still takes plenty of guts on her part, since even a queen could be killed for entering the king's presence unannounced, let alone trying to change his mind about matters of state.

Main theme

Amazingly—this is, after all, the Bible—God is not mentioned in the whole book of Esther. That doesn't mean God isn't working behind the scenes.

It's typical of Satan that, at a critical time like this, when the exiles are being allowed back to Jerusalem and the temple is being built, he tries to sneak a cruel plan in behind God's back. It doesn't work, though, thanks to Esther and her cousin Mordecai.

Central characters

King Xerxes, the incredibly powerful king of Persia

Esther, his young and beautiful Jewish queen

Haman, the evil schemer who wants to kill off the Jews

Mordecai, Esther's brave cousin who uncovers the plot

interesting bits

It's an exciting story, so get a good modern translation and just read it!

The Five Books

THE OLD

Genesis Exodus
Leviticus Numbers
Deuteronomy

Joshua Judges **Ruth**
1 Samuel 2 Samuel 1 Kings 2
Kings **1 Chronicles**
2 Chronicles Ezra Nehemiah
Esther

The Historical Books

ALL ACCESS

Backstage Pass

Job
Psalms
Proverbs
Ecclesiastes
Song of Songs

The Books of Poetry and Wisdom

TESTAMENT

Job **Psalms** Proverbs
Ecclesiastes Song
of Songs

Isaiah **Jeremiah**
Lamentations Ezekiel
Daniel Hosea Joel Amos Obadiah
Jonah Micah Nahum Habakkuk
Zephaniah Haggai Zechariah
Malachi

The Old Testament Prophets

The Books of
Poetry and Wisdom

Why are these books grouped together?

The Jewish people split their Old Testament into three sections: the law, the prophets (which include the history books), and the writings. The five books we're looking at now all come from the writings section of the Jewish Old Testament.

What is poetry?

"I wouldn't be caught dead with a poem in my hand. That's for snobs and wimps—not for me!"

When people talk like that, they're probably only thinking of a particular type of poetry and forgetting that song lyrics (what *is* a *wonderwall*?), limericks ("There was an old man from...") and nursery rhymes ("Hey diddle diddle") are poetry as well.

The ancient Israelites used poetry much more than we do today, and all the books in this section of the Bible include poetry. The intention was to make the books more memorable, more entertaining, and more full of feeling than ordinary writing often allows. Fortunately, this kind of poetry didn't rely too much on rhymes or precise rhythms, so we can still understand it when it's translated from the original language.

What does wisdom mean?

"It takes more than a few exams to make you wise. Real wisdom only comes to older people who have experienced life."

This was the thinking in Old Testament times. Gray hair was considered the greatest sign of wisdom because back then you must have done something right just to have lived that long. For this reason, the sayings and teachings of the wise were treasured and written down and then taught to young people like a sort of textbook on how to live life.

There are two types of wisdom writing in the books we're looking at: proverbs (in the book of Proverbs—duh), and reflection (see Job and Ecclesiastes).

Proverbs are short, sharp, often funny sayings with a point to make.

Reflective wisdom is deeper, more thoughtful, and often takes the form of a conversation (Job) or a long speech (Ecclesiastes).

Solomon

When it comes to wisdom, Solomon is the man. The Bible shows that his remarkable wisdom was a gift from God, but he made the most of his natural gift by some serious studying.

When he ruled, Israel was known as a center of science and thought, and wise men from around the world traveled there to teach and learn. Solomon and others learned all they could from the visiting wise men, then improved on this knowledge by applying to it the special things God taught them.

Solomon's name is sometimes attached as author to all three of the wisdom books. At the very least, we know he wrote some of the Proverbs and possibly Ecclesiastes.

Central characters
David

Psalms is the longest book in the Bible, and the main man behind it is David. His love of worshiping God through music is legendary, and some people think David brought together what might have been the world's first orchestra to aid the people in their worship.

After David's death, music became a very important part of worshiping God in the temple. So, though David certainly didn't write all the Psalms, his influence was very important.

The Book of
Nehemiah

A book for those who are suffering

First off . . .

What's the worst thing that ever happened to you? Is it failing an exam, waking up with a terrible case of zits, or something more serious?

It can be very confusing to believe in a good and all-powerful God and, then, have to suffer or watch other innocent people suffer. That's not a new problem, and it's one that's faced head-on in the book of Job.

Ground covered

There are bad days (Mondays for most of us), very bad days (drizzly Mondays when you realize you haven't done your homework), and very, very bad days (we're talking nothing-goes-right-and-even-the-dog-hates-me sort of days), but few of us have ever experienced bad days like Job experienced bad days.

Job was a very good and very wealthy man. Suddenly everything went wrong for him—his children were killed, all his wealth was wiped out, and his body was covered in ugly, painful skin erup-tions called boils (a fate I hope you never endure).

Some of Job's friends were convinced he must have done something wrong to have caused all this, but he maintained his innocence.

Main theme

Right at the end of the book, Job is privileged to speak to God. God does not answer his questions as to why these things happened. God simply shows his greatness and his justice.

In the end, Job realizes what's important is not knowing the answer, but knowing God.

But what about me?

As you read through Job, you'll see the impossibility of trying to understand the cause of every unfair thing that happens in the world. Like Job, we need to learn that our quest must be to find God, not to find an answer. The more we know God, the more certain we can be that he'll be fair in the end.

Interesting bits

The start of all the trouble—read Job 1:1–2:10
The Lord speaks to Job—read Job 38:1–40:2
Are these monsters dinosaurs?—read Job 40:15–41:34
The happy ending—read Job 42:10–17

The Book of
Proverbs

A book of timeless advice for living life

First off . . .

Some people are just naturally practical. At school they can be heard saying: "Like I'm ever really gonna need to know who was king of England in 1066... Besides, this is why God gave us the Internet."

If they wanted to read the Bible, Proverbs would be their book.

Ground covered

Some so-called geniuses can't even explain how to use the toilet without taking two hours and using overhead projectors and slides.

Not so the writers of Proverbs. This book is a collection of wisemen's teachings, boiled down to the smallest possible units. These short sayings are called proverbs, and they contain sound, practical advice on many aspects of life.

Short sayings summarize wise teaching and make the point better than many long sermons. What's more, unlike sermons, you can remember proverbs 30 minutes later.

sprouts with wings

Main theme

If you're building, you need foundations. If you don't have a foundation, your architectural masterpiece will make like a pancake in a very short space of time.

The wise men of Proverbs knew that wisdom also requires a firm foundation. The foundation they chose was *the fear of the Lord*. It was only if you already understood something of God and respected (feared) him that you would benefit from their teaching.

But what about me?

Advice on chariot racing or how to ride a camel wouldn't be of much use to us today. Fortunately, that's not what the proverbs are all about. Instead, they deal with timeless themes such as honesty, gossip, pride, loyalty, and greed.

interesting bits

A few peaches

The firm foundation—read Proverbs 9:10

When is a beautiful woman like a pig?
—read Proverbs 11:22

Some plums

Money often sprouts wings and flies off
—read Proverbs 23:4–5

An honest answer is like a kiss on the lips
—read Proverbs 24:26

The Book of
Psalms

A book for those who want to praise God every day

First off . . .

Can you imagine Christians singing Deliriou5? worship songs in 2,000 years' time? They'll be in their space suits up on Mars singing "Did You Feel the Mountains Tremble?" through their headset microphones.

I wonder if the writers of the book of Psalms knew their songs would be around for thousands of years and still used as a songbook by Christians and Jews alike.

Ground covered

If you went down the road to the local music store and asked for a single CD that brought together classical, country, dance, rap, swing, a capella, speed metal, folk, goth, and hip hop, the assistant would look at you rather strangely.

Yet in the book of Psalms, the 150 songs of worship to God are about as different as the music listed above. There are loud songs to be sung by massed choirs and big orchestras. There are quiet meditative songs to be sung by one person to

God. There are sad songs, as well as songs of celebration.

Main themes

God and life

It's impossible to pick one main theme out of the Psalms—they deal with every aspect of life and every possible emotion and feeling toward God. The Psalm writers rightly assumed that God is involved in all of these situations and wants to be part of every area of our lives.

This is a lyric, not a theology essay

What's the dumbest song lyric you've ever heard? There are some stupid ones, aren't there? But that doesn't always mean the songs aren't good or that you don't understand what the songwriter means. When you listen to a song, you don't expect to come away with a deeper understanding of nuclear physics, but you do expect to feel something.

In the same way, the writers of the Psalms were focusing on their feelings toward God rather than on theology. When the writers cry out for their enemies' babies to be dashed against rocks, this is obviously not something God would approve of, but it's in the Psalms because it shows honestly how people felt.

When you read the Psalms, be aware that these are song lyrics and not theology—don't feel like you need to copy everything that's said and done!

On the other, don't be afraid to express your full range of emotions to God. Clearly, he can take it.

Jesus in the Psalms

Royal Psalms (like 2, 72, and 110) speak of a king and spiritual leader so perfect that only Jesus could possibly match up. Other Psalms, particularly 22, describe the suffering that Jesus endured. As you read the Psalms, look out for the shadow of Jesus just behind the words, even though they were written hundreds of years before Jesus came to earth.

But what about me?

I hate those tongue-tied situations when you just don't know what to say. You stand there with your face hanging out, your mouth opening and closing stupidly, with no words coming out.

The Psalms can help us express ourselves to God. Not only can we look for a Psalm that fits what we want to say—and believe me, there's one for every occasion—the Psalms also show us it's okay to tell God everything. If you're angry, tell him. If you're sad, explain. If you're confused, lay it all out honestly.

interesting bits— six of the best

The world-famous "The Lord is my shepherd"—read Psalm 23

When you've messed up bad, try this—read Psalm 51

When life seems frightening, look here—read Psalm 91

The longest chapter in the Bible, but good—read Psalm 119

God knows and loves you—read Psalm 139

The last Psalm needs major decibels to work right—read Psalm 150

do you feel the mountains tremble?

Houston, we have a problem

The Book of Ecclesiastes

A book that's not afraid to look at the downside of life

First off . . .

According to the media, you and I are part of Generation X—or maybe Y—cynical and hopeless, we trust nothing and no one. That attitude is nothing new—the author of Ecclesiastes felt the same way.

Ground covered

If you had money to burn, a kingdom to rule, and hundreds of beautiful wives to keep you company, would you be happy? "Of course!" you cry!

Well, King Solomon wrote a book that focuses on all the unfairness, the cruelty, and the pointlessness in the world. Nowhere does he find anything that brings true happiness—not hard work or money or goodness. Even looking for fun gets boring after a time.

Main theme

So what's such a pessimistic book doing in the Bible? The truth is that much of what the writer outlines is true. Life is terribly unfair. (What did you and I do to deserve to be born in a relatively wealthy country?) The bottom line: none of the things he talks about in this book can make anyone truly happy.

But we must view the book of Ecclesiastes alongside the rest of the Bible. Then we can see how God's presence makes life worth living and God's justice puts all the unfairness of life in perspective.

rose-tinted specs

But what about me?

Sometimes Christians are accused of looking at the world through rose-colored glasses—pretending life is easier and fairer than it really is. It's possible to enjoy our relationship with God and our hope of heaven so much we forget other people's difficulties and pain. A quick reading of the book of Ecclesiastes is good medicine for this problem.

Interesting bits

Setting the tone (what's the point?)—read Ecclesiastes 1:1–11
Is there a time for everything?—read Ecclesiastes 3:1–8
Face difficult times with friends—read Ecclesiastes 4:9–12
Start serving God while you're young—read Ecclesiastes 11:7–12:5
A final word of advice—read Ecclesiastes 12:9–14

The Book of
The Song of Songs

A book that gives a God's-eye-view of sex

First off . . .

There are two kinds of romantics—those who admit they're romantics and those who hide it. Generally the members of the first group are girls and the second are boys. Yes, boys are romantics, too; they just hide it. The fact that this book is in the Bible proves God is a romantic too.

Ground covered

Reading the Song of Songs is like reading somebody else's love letters—naughty but nice. It's a steamy collection of songs or poems sung by two lovers to each other. They sing about their attraction to each other, their physical desire for each other's bodies, and their longing to be together. It's hard to be sure, but the man may have been King Solomon, and the woman may have been a beautiful young girl whom he added to his collection of wives.

Main theme

Many people have tried very hard over the centuries to make this book mean something they thought was really spiritual, but it's still not totally clear whether this Bible book is simply about sexual love or whether it all has hidden deep spiritual meaning.

But what about me?

We live in a sex-crazed world. Advertisers use sex to sell everything from diamonds to washing machines—and what could be less sexy than a washing machine?

This book helps us to put sex in its proper place. It's a wonderful gift that God finds beautiful. But sex belongs in committed marriage—not on billboards or in films, casual relationships, and one-night stands. These things rob sex of its value as a precious gift, handmade by God.

interesting bits

The man describes his bride—read Song of Songs 4:1–7

The woman describes her husband—read Song of Songs 5:10–16

79

The Five Books

Genesis Exodus
Leviticus Numbers
Deuteronomy

THE OLD

Joshua Judges **Ruth**
1 Samuel 2 Samuel 1 Kings 2
Kings **1 Chronicles**
2 Chronicles Ezra Nehemiah
Esther

The Historical Books

The Books of
Poetry and Wisdom

TESTAMENT

Job **Psalms** Proverbs
Ecclesiastes Song
of Songs

Isaiah **Jeremiah**
Lamentations Ezekiel
Daniel Hosea Joel Amos Obadiah
Jonah Micah Nahum Habakkuk
Zephaniah Haggai Zechariah
Malachi

Isaiah
Jeremiah
Lamentations
Ezekiel
Daniel
Hosea
Joel
Amos
Obadiah
Jonah
Micah
Nahum
Habakkuk
Zephaniah
Haggai
Zechariah
Malachi

The Old Testament
Prophets

81

The Old Testament Prophets

Who were they?

Walking down a dark street late at night, on your way home from a party, you see a group walking toward you that makes you want to cross to the other side of the street—just to be on the safe side.

If you saw the Old Testament prophets walking toward you, you'd probably want to do the same thing. These were real characters, men called by God from various walks of life to be his spokesmen. It wasn't an easy, popular, or safe job, and you had to be a certain type of man.

Would you like a job as a prophet?

PROPHET
REQUIRED QUALIFICATIONS:
ACADEMIC
none
BACKGROUND
farmers, priests, minor royals, all welcome
CHARACTER
must be strong independent type

must be able to stand up under threats

must be willing to die for what you believe

must be holy enough to be close to God

must not care what other people think of you

Still think you're the person for the job? Then read on.

What will I have to say?

"Palm readers don't get death threats," you might be saying. "The man who does the horoscopes on morning TV is a nice, friendly guy. I can't imagine him being hated and threatened. What did the Old Testament prophets do to be so unpopular?"

The predictions of the prophets weren't the nice comfortable "You'll meet a tall dark stranger" horoscope type or the intriguingly weird predictions of modern doomsayers. The prophets spoke strong words from God to the people of the time, generally calling them to change their ways and return to God.

How will I know what to say?

When you know people really well, you know what really sets them off and what really makes them happy. To be a prophet, you had to have that sort of close relationship with God. The prophets knew and understood him better than anyone else alive in their times.

They understood how God expected things to be, and God spoke to them about what was wrong in their societies. Their prophecies weren't half-mad ramblings. They were carefully constructed sermons and messages, preached with great power.

But do I get to predict the future?

You'd better believe it, but not as often as you might think. God is Lord of all of history, and when it suits his purposes it's not a problem for him to reveal what's going to happen to his spokesmen the prophets.

But he doesn't do it just because he can or to give people a thrill. God only allows his prophets to predict future events for a purpose. Normally this is either to warn the nation of something bad about to happen, or to give them hope after something bad has happened.

Studying the Old Testament prophets in the Bible

It's a crazy world we live in. Did you know perfectly boring, respectable academics in our universities are now saying time travel is, at least theoretically, possible. They have absolutely no idea how you can do it—although they're certain it won't be in a stainless steel, DeLorean two-seater—but they think it can be done. I can't wait!

When we read the words of the Old Testament prophets, we're traveling 2,500 years back in time. This has advantages and disadvantages. Positively, we can see how good their predictions were, but negatively, we find it hard to understand the relevance of what they had to say when we know nothing about the situation at the time.

In the next chapters we have pulled together groups of prophets who prophesied at approximately the same time about the same events. This means we will not go in exactly the same order as the Bible lists them, but this should make what they had to say easier to understand.

The Books of
Isaiah, Micah, Amos, and Hosea

Prophets before the fall of the Northern Kingdom

The times they lived in

Enemies

There were some big bullies knocking around Israel at this time—the Assyrians. Their home and empire were in the north, but they had the muscle were to control the lands to the south as well, including the northern and southern kingdoms of Israel.

They were the superpower of the time, and they knew it. They just loved throwing their weight around.

Politics

The big question with bullies is deciding when to stand up to them. "Is this a good day to risk losing my teeth, or should I just hand over the lunch money again?" was roughly the decision the kings of the northern kingdom had to make.

After forking over their lunch money for quite a while, they made the brave (but really foolish) decision to stand up to the Assyrians. Faster than you could say, "Not this time buddy," the bullies swept down from the north like an avalanche, and the northern kingdom was knocked flat.

Lifestyle

Strangely enough, right up to the very moment the Assyrians planted their Doc Martens in the middle of the Israelites' backs, plenty of the inhabitants of the northern kingdom were turning a nice profit.

Being controlled by another nation might not be fun, but it was good for the economy. The rich people got richer by the minute and practically fought each other for the privilege of building next door to the Beverly Hillbillies.

At the same time, the poor people just got poorer. While this didn't bother the rich people, it bothered God and his prophets—a lot!

Religion

"If it feels good, do it" was the normal attitude to religion at this time.

The people of the northern kingdom thought religion was just an excuse for national holidays every once in a while.

Just for giggles, they mixed in any parts of other religions that seemed like fun. God was not amused.

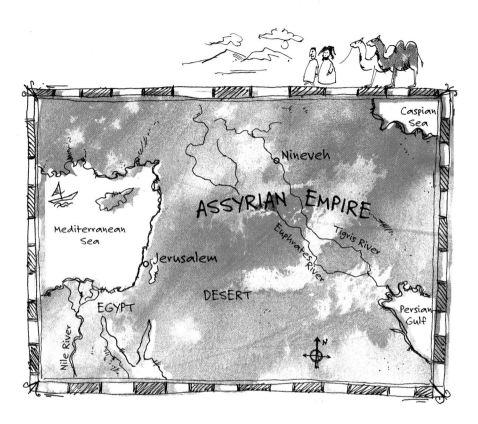

MAP OF THE ASSYRIAN EMPIRE

The Prophet isaiah

*A book for those who
need hope for the future*

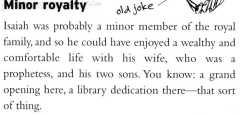
old joke

Minor royalty

Isaiah was probably a minor member of the royal family, and so he could have enjoyed a wealthy and comfortable life with his wife, who was a prophetess, and his two sons. You know: a grand opening here, a library dedication there—that sort of thing.

Instead, Isaiah spent his life speaking God's often unpopular words to his nation. Eventually Isaiah was killed for his truthfulness when the wicked King Manasseh had him sawed in half (this was no Fox network special; when they cut to a commercial, Isaiah was really dead).

Sweet and sour

I love a good sandwich—fresh bread, pickle, anchovies, and lots of strawberry jam! Just kidding; I'm not all that crazy about pickles.

Isaiah's message was a bit like a strange sandwich. The first slice of bread (chapters 1–35) was very bitter for the people to eat because Isaiah prophesied the judgment that was coming.

The bottom slice of bread (chapters 40–66) was really sweet, more like cake than bread, because Isaiah talked of hope for the future after the judgment.

The bit in the middle (chapters 36–39) told how God delivered King Hezekiah and the city of Jerusalem from the mighty Assyrian King Sennacherib.

But what about me?

So many things in life start off exciting and then just fizzle out over time. Just think of relationships, your favorite football team's season, and television series. It's different with God. With God, things get better and more exciting toward the end.

We see this in the book of Isaiah. With God, judgment is never the end of the story, only the beginning. As one of the Psalms says: "His anger lasts only a moment, but his favor lasts a lifetime" (Psalm 30:5).

Remember that about God the next time you feel depressed with life, or when you feel you've failed him. With God, the best is always yet to come!

interesting bits

The story of Isaiah's call—read Isaiah 6:1–13

A popular reading for Christmas—read Isaiah 9:1–7

A picture of the end of the world—read Isaiah 24:1–23

The Prophet Micah

A book about what makes God happy

Brave bumpkin

Micah was as poor and unconnected as Isaiah was rich and well-bred. This poor country bumpkin bravely prophesied what God was going to do to the arrogant and wealthy capital cities of the two kingdoms of Israel.

No more scam

The Israelites had worked out what they thought was a wonderful scam: "Here's the deal. You know how when we sin, we offer sacrifices to God to pay for them, right? Well, why don't we sin as much as we possibly can, then offer God lots and lots of sacrifices. Then everyone's happy. God gets lots of sacrifices, and we get to do whatever we like!"

The false prophets, who got paid commission on the number of animals sacrificed, said this was fine, but God made his real feelings known through Micah.

God wasn't interested in the big religious shows the people put on, especially when they began to offer human sacrifices. He was interested in how they lived their normal lives and how they treated him and other people.

But what about me?

No doubt we've all tried something similar to the plan above. We think we can live as we please all week as long as we ask God to forgive us in church on Sunday.

But God's not interested in how we look when we worship on Sunday or how spiritual we sound when we pray. God's interested in how we live every day of the week.

interesting bits

God's requirements—read Micah 6:6–8

nice cardigan

The Prophet Amos

A book to remind us never to forget less fortunate people

Hey you, uh, bad dudes there

Imagine being told by God to stand outside the gates of the roughest school in town and preach to the toughest gangs coming out.

That was Amos' mission from God. He was just a quiet shepherd and gardener from the hills in the southern kingdom, but God sent him to preach in the religious center of the bigger, badder northern kingdom.

You selfish cows, you

Nothing makes people feel better than a bit of flattery, and what Amos had to say was nothing like a bit of flattery. He started out by calling the wealthy women of Israel cows and finished by telling them they were going to be dragged away by their enemies on hooks (which was how the Assyrians led away their captives).

Amos focused on one of the many things that made God angry with the northern kingdom—the way the rich treated the poor. The rich cheated the poor, they sold them bread at ridiculously high prices, and they bribed judges to keep them quiet.

Amos prophesied that God was going to judge this cruelty, and he was right. Just 20 years later the Assyrians invaded and destroyed the whole land, taking all the wealthy people into exile.

But what about me?

God cares about poor and suffering people. If we want to make God angry, there's no better way than treating such people unfairly. If we want to be like God, we need to help people less fortunate than ourselves.

interesting bits

God's thoughts stated plainly—read Amos 3:13–4:5, 5:11–15

nice dress

moo

stack heels

miner prophet

The Prophet Hosea

A book that shows that no one loves you like God loves you

Marry a *who*?!

Hosea was told by God to marry a prostitute. I'll repeat that in case you missed it—God told Hosea to marry a prostitute. Not only that, later, after she left him to live with other lovers and return to her old work as a prostitute, Hosea was told to take her back again.

But why?

I'll always love you

Hosea's was a message of God's love, even for his horribly sinful people. Hosea used his own relationship as an example.

The people of Israel were like an unfaithful wife, and God was her loyal husband. The people ran off following other gods, and they were going to be punished for this. But God still loved them and would always take them back if they returned to him.

But what about me?

The prophet Hosea shows us God's incredible love. As humans we will never know another love—not even from our parents or our wives or husbands—to compare with the love God has for us. His is a love we have never deserved, and so we can never do anything to stop him from loving us. Nothing! Ever!

interesting bits

The story of Hosea and Gomer—read Hosea 1:1–9, 3:1–3

God will win back Israel's love—read Hosea 2:14–23

God has always loved Israel—read Hosea 11:1–11

The Books of

Jeremiah, Lamentations, Nahum, Habakkuk, and Zephaniah

Prophets before the fall of Judah

The times they lived in

Enemies

Talk about high-pressure situations. The people of the southern kingdom must have thought they were caught in some kind of international nutcracker—right between the two greatest empires of the time. Egypt from the south was at war with Babylon in the north—and it looked like Judah was going to be the battleground.

Politics

It's difficult to remain neutral when a war is being fought in your garden, so the big political question was which side to fight on? Egypt or Babylon—Babylon or Egypt?

In the end, Judah sided with Egypt—a big mistake that brought the full wrath of the Babylonian empire down on their heads. Before these prophets stopped speaking, Judah had been destroyed and its people carried into captivity.

Lifestyle

As you might imagine, these were tough times for the people of Judah. No one likes being caught between a rock and a hard place. To make things worse, Babylon was an even nastier piece of work than Assyria, who had led the people of the northern kingdom off with rings through their noses.

There was also a proud belief that nothing bad could happen to Jerusalem, God's holy city. The priests and the king said, "Don't worry, nothing will happen!" The prophets said, "Oh yes it will!" The people knew whom they wanted to believe, but they weren't quite sure who was telling the truth.

Religion

You'd think seeing the northern kingdom destroyed as the prophets predicted would make the people of Judah turn back to God.

Well, for a while this did happen. Under the good King Josiah, there was a mass revival in the southern kingdom. But it didn't last, and soon the people were back to their worship of other gods, forgetting the one true God.

MAP OF THE BABYLONIAN EMPIRE

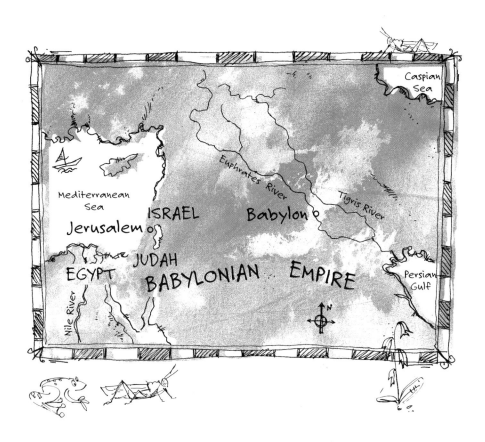

The Prophet Jeremiah

A book that predicts a new kind of relationship with God

Branded

There's nothing so despised and low as a traitor. What could be worse than selling out your friends to save your own skin or to make a buck?

Throughout his life, Jeremiah was branded as a traitor and a spy for the Babylonians. Eventually he was arrested, whipped, imprisoned, and thrown into a muddy pit to die. He wasn't a traitor, but he did know God was using the Babylonians, and it was useless to resist them.

Bad news, good news

Jeremiah followed up his message of judgment with a message of hope. It was a hope that one day God would make a new agreement with his people that wouldn't be based on keeping laws and sacrificing animals but would involve a personal relationship with God.

But what about me?

Off goes the alarm, announcing another exhausting day at school. "I'm just way too tired to read my Bible or pray—I'll wait until tomorrow."

Sometimes keeping in touch with God can seem like hard work, but we need to remember how good we've got it. We have the privilege of living under the new agreement with God that Jeremiah prophesied.

interesting bits

God calls Jeremiah to be his prophet
—read Jeremiah 1:1–19

Jeremiah can't stop speaking God's word
—read Jeremiah 20:7–9

God will make a new agreement
—read Jeremiah 31:31–34

Jeremiah is treated like a traitor, but he's proved right in the end—read Jeremiah 36:1–40:6

Lamentations

A book that mourns the destruction of a city

Lamentations are sad poems written to describe and mourn the destruction of Jerusalem by the Babylonians. The news-report style shows they were written by an eyewitness.

The Prophet Nahum

A lesson about pride and humility

Psst...hey buddy...you're dead meat

Nahum was a bit of an undercover operative. We know absolutely nothing about him, except he was presumably from the nation of Judah. God's mission for him was to prophesy to Nineveh, the capital city of Assyria.

Basically his message was, "All right, time's up! God's used you to judge the northern kingdom; now it's your turn, and you're going to be destroyed yourselves."

No wonder he operated under cover!

Too big for their britches

Sometimes people get a little too big for their britches and have to be taken down a notch or two. Just because God allowed the Assyrians to destroy Israel, they were under the impression they were bigger than God. Wrong!

Nahum was assigned by God to prophesy the Assyrians destruction because it was important that they know God is the big dog.

But what about me?

Have you ever known someone who is really good-looking—but totally unattractive because he or she is sickeningly proud about it? Pride is so obnoxious.

God feels the same way. He helps humble people, but sooner or later he gives proud people—like the Assyrians—what they deserve. If we know what's good for us, we'll make sure we stay—get—humble.

Interesting bits

Awesome description of God coming to judge—read Nahum 1:1–11

When Nineveh falls, everyone will rejoice—read Nahum 3:18–19

The Prophet Habakkuk

An example for us when we're confused about life

What gives, God?

Right at the top of my to-do list when I get to heaven, even before a quick, self-propelled flight around the universe or watching the videotapes of creation, is to have a little Q & A session with God. There are some things I just don't understand. Habakkuk also had a few tough questions for God.

Wait and see

Habakkuk was upset at the way things were going. Evil nations like the Babylonians and Assyrians were having a whale of a time, and good people seemed to suffer most.

"Look, God," he said. "You've got some explaining to do."

Since he was a prophet, and no doubt far more spiritual than you or me, Habakkuk got some answers from God—but probably not the ones he was hoping for.

God said, "Be patient, and you'll see."

But what about me?

Habakkuk's final response is a perfect example of what God calls all of us to do when we don't understand. Habakkuk declares in a beautiful prayer that no matter how confused he is, no matter how bad things look, he'll trust in God anyway.

interesting bits

The brave prayer of Habakkuk—read Habakkuk 3:1–19

HEAVEN TO-DO LIST:
creation ✓
universe ✓
England World
Cup 1966 ✓
Questions + answers ✓
Find where I left
that retainer

The Prophet Zephaniah

A book that reminds us that God doesn't exist just to make us happy

Cousin Zeph

Another wannabe member of the royal family, Zephaniah was a distant cousin to King Josiah in whose reign he prophesied. Possibly due to Zephaniah's bold prophesying, as well as that of Jeremiah, there was something of a national revival, and the southern kingdom turned back toward God.

Sadly, it was too little, too late—judgment was still on its way.

A Club Fed holiday

The lottery—imagine the elation, the excitement, the joy, if your numbers actually come up. But your jaw might drop and your feelings would do a very abrupt U-turn if it was then announced that this week's prize was a very long prison sentence.

That's pretty much the effect Zephaniah's message had on the people of Judah. They had a belief that at one point the Day of the Lord would come and God would destroy their enemies and elevate them to the position of greatness they thought they deserved.

"Oh, no!" said Zephaniah. "The day's coming, but rather than joy, there will be judgment of your sins."

But what about me?

God—the sweet old grandfather in the clouds or a heavenly Santa Claus who gives me whatever I want.

Those attitudes are the modern equivalent of the expectations of the people of the southern kingdom. Like them, we sometimes need to be reminded God doesn't exist just to give us what we want. He is the Master of the Universe, and we need to treat him with real respect.

Interesting bits

How the Day of the Lord will really be— read Zephaniah 1:14–18

Not everyone will be destroyed; some will live to rejoice and serve God again—read Zephaniah 3:6–20

The Books of
Ezekiel and Daniel

Prophets in exile

The times they lived in

Enemies

Remember the old joke, "What do you call a 500-pound gorilla with a machine gun?" The answer is, "Sir!"

The time for calling the Babylonians *enemies* had passed—they were definitely in charge. It was now a matter of being as nice to the gorilla as possible, hoping he wouldn't select you to join him for target practice—as the target.

Politics

Sometimes people just don't get the message.

At first you're kind: "I'm really sorry, but I'm busy that night." Then you're clear: "You're a good friend, but I don't want to go out with you." Then you have to be brutal: "You're ugly, my goldfish has more personality, and I'd become a nun before I'd go out with you. Get lost!"

The people of the southern kingdom just didn't get the message that the Babylonians had won. The Babylonians first took a small group of hostages, then they took more captives, and finally King Nebuchadnezzar went to war and completely destroyed Jerusalem.

Only when almost the whole nation was taken into captivity did the people realize they'd lost.

Lifestyle in exile

If your family ever had to move because of a parent's change of job, you might have some idea how the people felt about going into exile. They were devastated about leaving their homes and everything they knew, and they were scared of what they might find when they got to their new location.

For most it wasn't too bad. The cream of Judah's society was even allowed to live in the royal palaces. Only the most unlucky were made slaves of the Babylonians.

Religion

Painful situations can make us doubt all we have always believed about God. The exile was a time like that for the people of Judah.

The prophets explained to the people that it wasn't because God was weak that they had been defeated, but because they walked away from him. Now that the worst had happened, the prophets began offering hope to the people by prophesying that one day God would take his people back to their land and things would be better than ever.

The Prophet Ezekiel

A book that encourages us to stay close to God

All that training, and now just an alien

Some people know incredibly early in life what they want to be when they grow up. They're dressing up in firefighter uniforms or teaching classes composed of dolls and teddy bears, all by the age of five.

Ezekiel was like that. Even as a kid he was very dedicated, and he trained to become a priest in God's holy temple in Jerusalem. Unfortunately, his career plans took a serious hit when King Nebuchadnezzar diminished job opportunities by reducing the temple to a heap of rubble.

When he was roughly 20 years old, Ezekiel was one of many taken to Babylon as prisoners of war. That was the end of his childhood dreams. He somehow managed to keep his faith, and five years later God called Ezekiel to be his prophet to the people living in exile in Babylon.

During this time he saw the most incredible vision of the holiness and glory of the Lord. Ezekiel couldn't have been jolted more if he had plugged his finger into an electric socket. He fell flat on his face and was in shock for the next seven days.

Bizarre object lessons

I have a gift for forgetting sermons. It doesn't matter how good I think they are while I'm listening—15 minutes later I can barely remember who was speaking.

Ezekiel was the perfect speaker for people like me because God often told him to act out his messages to the people. These weren't just funny little skits, though. Some of them were in very bad taste.

At one point, God told Ezekiel to cook his food over a fire whose fuel was human excrement. That's right—burning poop. Ezekiel thought this was going a bit further than was absolutely necessary to make the point, so he persuaded God to let him cook over animal dung instead—as if that's a lot better!

Other times he had to cut off his hair or lay on one side for hundreds of days. Once he had to act out someone being taken into exile (no problem, he knew all about that experience) to show that soon everyone would be in exile.

The temple? Glad you mentioned it

It's amazing how people with a real passion for either something or someone manage to bring it into practically every conversation. "It's funny you should mention food because my hamster Sophie—she is *so* sweet—has a real partiality to this new pet food I found. Blah, blah, blah."

Well, Ezekiel's passion was the temple. It might be rubble now, but he dreamed of a time when it would be rebuilt and more wonderful than ever. The people couldn't understand how the temple could have been destroyed if God was living there.

"Ah," said Ezekiel. "It's because he wasn't home."

That might sound like a stupid explanation to us, but it's exactly what God showed to Ezekiel in a vision. God had been so disgusted with the evil things the people were doing in his holy temple that he simply left. The people were so far away from God they didn't even notice he was gone.

God also gave Ezekiel a vision showing that he would return to the temple.

But what about me?

Have you ever thought: "God, where on earth are you? I need you, and you're not here."

Fortunately, under the new agreement God never actually leaves us. But it's possible for us to walk away from him for a period of time and then suddenly wonder where he is when we need him.

If we want to avoid the experience of the people of the southern kingdom, where God left and they didn't even know until something bad happened, we need to be sure we keep close to God all the time.

interesting bits

Ezekiel's call to be a prophet—read Ezekiel 1:1–3:15

God's presence leaves the temple—read Ezekiel 10:1–22

Dead skeletons become alive—read Ezekiel 37:1–14

God returns to the new temple—read Ezekiel 43:1–12

Ezekiel

animal dung (fortunately)—

The Prophet Daniel

A book to encourage Christians to stand strong for God

Mr. Perfect Prophet

In every school there's sure to be someone who turns you green with envy. She seems too good to be true and makes everybody else look stupid, ugly, unathletic, and totally ungifted in comparison.

The prophet Daniel must have seemed like that to the people he grew up with. As a young boy from a wealthy family, he was taken to Babylon when king Nebuchadnezzar took the first group of hostages. Daniel was chosen, along with several others, to live in the king's palace and be trained and educated to serve him.

Because of his many talents, Daniel soon became popular and trusted, especially when God added the special gift of interpreting dreams to his already glowing résumé.

By the time he reached old age, Daniel, who had been brought to Babylon as a prisoner of war from an enemy country, had become the right-hand man of the Babylonian king.

Weird dreams

The first six chapters of Daniel tell amazing stories about the 70 years Daniel lived in Babylon. They were written to encourage the people living in captivity in Babylon. They show how God will protect them if they keep their faith in him.

The second part of Daniel is a whole new ball game. If your little brother or sister had dreams like this, they'd run crying to your parents' bedroom every night. Even Daniel admits some of these visions and dreams turned him white with fear.

The dreams are full of weird beasts, monsters, and people that talk and crush and destroy. The particular emphasis is on different empires of the world and on God's kingdom, which is greater than them all.

But what about me?

Most of our schools may not be Babylon exactly, but they are foreign territory for us as Christians. The stories of Daniel and his friends should encourage us to stand up for God in hostile situations.

interesting bits

Daniel's first experiences in Babylon—read Daniel 1:1–21

The idol and the fiery furnace—read Daniel 3:1–30

Daniel's not a lion's dinner—read Daniel 6:1–28

DANIEL

The Books of

Haggai, Zechariah, and Malachi

Prophets after the exile

The time they lived in

Enemies

Nothing lasts forever, not only good things like the Christmas holiday, but also bad things like math lessons.

The evil Babylonian empire didn't last forever either. In the end God made sure it was judged for its sins, and it was conquered by the Persians.

The Persians were far more humane rulers, and they allowed that the Babylonians' captives to go home.

Politics

Under the Persians, some of the people of Judah were allowed to return home under the leadership of a man called Zerubbabel, grandson of one of the last kings of Judah.

Lifestyle

When they talked about their freedom on the way home, around the campfires with the camels snoring in the background, it seemed so exciting. They couldn't wait to see what God was going to do when they returned to their own land.

But they hadn't counted on how hard things were going to be for them. It's no small thing to rebuild a country from scratch, and often it was difficult to get a hold of even the basics, like food and clothes. Also there was a lot of opposition from the people who had ruled the land since they left, who didn't want to lose their power—naturally.

All in all, it wasn't quite the wonderful homecoming the people imagined for so many years.

Religion

The people started off with great enthusiasm for God who allowed them to return from captivity. They had all the right intentions.

The outward sign of this was how fast they set about trying to rebuild God's temple, but soon the opposition and the hardship got to them and they began to slack off. They started to think this living-in-your-own-country-worshiping-your-own-God thing wasn't all it was cracked up to be. Their work on the temple slowed, then came to a complete halt.

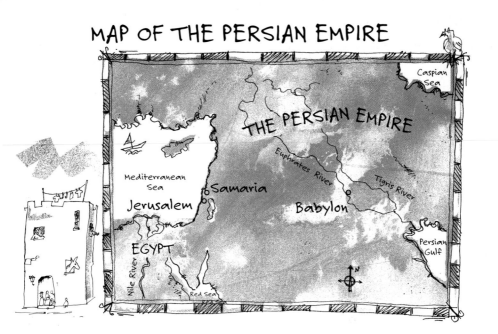

MAP OF THE PERSIAN EMPIRE

Caspian Sea

THE PERSIAN EMPIRE

Euphrates River

Tigris River

Mediterranean Sea

Samaria

Jerusalem

Babylon

EGYPT

Nile River

Red Sea

Persian Gulf

N

The Prophet Haggai

*A book that teaches us
to put God first in our lives*

Welcome home

Haggai returned home from exile some time after the first group. As he neared Jerusalem, he got more and more excited about the prospect of seeing the great city he had heard so much about, especially the magnificent new temple he heard had been built.

When he arrived, all he found was a building site. What's more, he could tell no work had been done in a very long time. "What went wrong?" he asked.

First things first

Life is all about setting priorities. "Is it more important that I do my history homework or watch 'Animaniacs'? No contest, cartoons are a far higher priority."

"Should I save this money to give in the offering at church or buy a pair of jeans? No contest. Putting new denim on my behind is much more important than putting a new roof on the church—isn't it?"

The people were busy building their own houses and were no longer concerned about God's house. Haggai told them they had their priorities all wrong. The reason they were struggling was because they weren't putting God first.

But what about me?

That's a lesson we all need to learn. When we put God first in our lives, whether it's by doing a morning quiet time or putting money into an offering, things will tend to go much better in other areas of our lives.

interesting bits

Encouragement to build the temple—read Haggai 1:1–15

A personal prophecy for Zerubbabel—read Haggai 2:22–23

The Prophet Zechariah

A book that predicts the life and death of Jesus

A prophet who was also a priest

"Now, look boys, it's like this. I'm a priest, right? That's how I earn my bread and butter. Well, I can't do any *priesting* until you hurry up and finish building the temple. So get a move on!"

Zechariah was from a family of priests who returned to Jerusalem. He joined Haggai in encouraging the people to keep working on the temple.

More importantly, God allowed him to look further into the future to an event even more significant than the rebuilding—the coming of God's Messiah whom we know to be Jesus.

Visions galore

The first part of Zechariah is a series of visions that all relate to the temple. In the second section we see many references to Jesus hundreds of years before his birth.

First we rejoice because he will enter Jerusalem riding on a donkey—a sign his reign will be peaceful, not warlike. Then we read the prophecy that he will be pierced, and people will mourn for him as if for a lost son or daughter. Also, we're told God will provide a fountain that will cleanse people from sin and impurity. We know now the fountain is Jesus' blood.

interesting bits

Read Zechariah chapters 9–14.

The Prophet Malachi

A book for when you're disappointed by God

So what's the expiration date on prophecies?

Malachi prophesied almost 100 years after Haggai and Zechariah. The words of those two earlier prophets had been listened to, and the temple was rebuilt—but still the prosperity and wonderful times the returned people of Judah expected God to give them had not actually happened. It was always going to be tomorrow, and tomorrow never came.

The people began to think God and his prophets had been stringing them along, promising a lot but never delivering the goods. They began to get slack about their worship and their relationship with God. Frankly, they were disappointed.

God hasn't forgotten you

God called Malachi to speak to the people, to show them he hadn't forgotten them.

First Malachi says, "Remember the good things God has done for you." For the Israelites this meant comparing themselves with other nations who had been taken by Babylon into captivity but who had not been allowed to return home.

Then Malachi said, "Keep making the effort. Keep treating God right, and the good times will come again."

But what about me?

It's not unusual to feel let down by God when bad things happen. We have a very different perspective than God, and we don't understand the way he works in our lives sometimes.

When we feel like that, then we, like the people of Judah, tend to slack off in our relationship with God and worship of him. But we need to do the opposite. We should trust him and spend time with him, so he can help us through the hard times.

interesting bits

The people aren't wholehearted—read Malachi 1:6–14

The people rob God—read Malachi 3:6–18

The final words of the Old Testament—read Malachi 4:4–6

The Books of
Joel, Obadiah, and Jonah

The timeless prophets

At least two of these three prophets are very hard to place in terms of their time in history. This doesn't matter, though, since the messages they speak are as relevant to us today as they were when they were written—whenever that was.

The Prophet Joel

A book that challenges us to change before it's too late

The swarm

You think your big brother eats a lot. Let me tell you eating Big Macs in a single mouthful is nothing compared to the appetite of the swarm of locusts that swept through the southern kingdom. They ate all the crops and destroyed everything in their path. They left the people penniless and in danger of starving.

Joel took the example of this terrible, natural catastrophe and used it as an object lesson to speak about being in relationship with God.

Big-time horror

Joel told the people what the locusts had done to them was just a picture of a far more terrible day in the future when God would judge sinful people. God's armies would march through the land like the locusts, only far more powerful and terrifying.

It wasn't all bad news, though. Joel knew this horror could be averted if the people would repent and turn back to God. If they did this, they would see great things from God.

One of Joel's prophecies was fulfilled in the New Testament when the Holy Spirit was poured out upon the disciples at Pentecost.

interesting bits

God's terrible army—read Joel 2:1–11

The people should repent before God—read Joel 2:12–17

God promises his Spirit for all people—read Joel 2:28–32

The Prophet Obadiah

A book with lessons on how we should treat other people

Sibling rivalry

Obadiah prophesied against a nation called Edom, and it wasn't a nice prophecy at all.

The Edomites were distant relatives of the Israelites, but the two nations hated each other and were always fighting. Recently, the Edomites had gloated over Israel's troubles and had actually assisted an enemy nation in attacking Israel—just to make a buck.

God sent Obadiah to tell the Edomites they were going to be judged for that behavior.

Nowhere to hide

The Edomites thought their city was invincible—hidden in the mountains and approachable only through a narrow gorge in which enemy soldiers could be killed at will.

"Don't count on it," said God through Obadiah. "I'm bigger than that, and you won't escape as easily as you think."

Sure enough, Edom was totally destroyed.

But what about me?

Obadiah's message is sobering for all of us: don't be happy when someone you have a grudge against gets in trouble.

God is concerned even with the way we treat our enemies, and we tend to end up being treated the same way we treat others.

Remember that the next time you're tempted to laugh when your worst enemy gets embarrassed in class.

But what about me?

Come on, read the whole thing—it's only 21 verses. Then you can say you've read a complete book of the Bible in one sitting!

The Prophet Jonah

A book for those who need to be warned about selfishness

Fish story

"Well, sir, I can offer you a berth on the *Queen Elizabeth 2* next Wednesday, but if you're really desperate there's still some room in the stomach of Moby Dick, who departs for Nineveh first thing tomorrow morning. We'll supply a plug for your nose since you'll be sharing the space with two tons of rotting tuna."

Everyone has heard of Jonah and his unusual mode of transport, but few of us know what was actually going on in this story.

See Jonah pout

God told Jonah to go and preach to the Assyrians in their capital city of Nineveh, to tell them God was going to judge them for their wickedness. Jonah told God this wasn't a good plan because—

1. They didn't like Israelites, especially not preachy ones.

2. They might escape the judgment if they knew it was coming.

So Jonah ran away—but as we all know, it wasn't for long.

But what about me?

Jonah's message to the Assyrians was repent or be judged, but the message of the whole book is about selfishness.

Jonah was concerned only for his own skin and his own country, but God is bigger than that. He is concerned for all the peoples and nations of the world.

Christians also need to remember God isn't our personal genie who is only there to make things run smoothly for us and our friends. He is concerned about everyone—even our enemies—and our job is to work for him wherever he calls us.

But what about me?

It's the fishy bit—read Jonah 1:14–2:10

God teaches Jonah a lesson—read Jonah 4:1–11

Don't look at me! Look at him!

Sounds like someone who's been caught doing something suspicious, doesn't it? He's standing there uncomfortably, looking extremely guilty, and he's desperately trying to shift the blame by pointing to someone else.

Well, for one thing it's rude to point—but that's exactly what I'm trying to do with this book. Let me explain.

Every author dreams of having a best seller. Imagine, being up there in the top 10 with the new John Grisham blockbuster, the revealing memoirs of an aging politician, and a book of exotic recipes from the TV chef du jour. Interviews on television, invitations to top literary lunches, and Steven Spielberg knocking on the door, begging to turn this masterpiece into a Hollywood hit.

Sounds great, and maybe one day it'll happen. But not with this book! You see, I'd be more than happy if you forget this book once you've read it.

"What did you say?"

Yes, that's right. The only reason this book has been written is to point you to another book, a much, much better book—*the* book.

Once you've put this book down, you might say: "Hmm, that was good. I laughed a little, learned a lot. Yes, I enjoyed that. Now I can start on that mystery novel." But that would be the wrong thing to say!

Yes, of course, read that mystery novel. But if this book hasn't made you want to go to the Bible as well, then I've failed miserably and I might as well have spent my days watching "Gilligan's Island."

Come on, dig into the Bible. It's exciting, challenging, life-changing. And you'll find the Bible is a book that points as well. It points to a person—a powerful and loving person, who has a plan for the human race and wants us to be part of it.

Now, I wonder who that person could be. Any ideas?

Hey, don't look at me! Look at him!

Old Testament books in alphabetical order

Amos, 84, 88

1 Chronicles, 64

2 Chronicles, 64

Daniel, 96, 98

Deuteronomy, 50

Ecclesiastes, 78

Esther, 69

Exodus, 46

Ezekiel, 96, 97

Ezra, 66

Genesis, 44

Habakkuk, 90, 94

Haggai, 100, 101

Hosea, 84, 89

Isaiah, 84, 86

Jeremiah, 90, 92

Job, 74

Joel, 104

Jonah, 104, 106

Joshua, 56

Judges, 58

1 Kings, 62

2 Kings, 62

Lamentations, 90, 93

Leviticus, 48

Malachi, 100, 103

Micah, 84, 87

Nahum, 90, 93

Nehemiah, 68

Numbers, 49

Obadiah, 104, 105

Proverbs, 75

Psalms, 76

Ruth, 59

1 Samuel, 60

2 Samuel, 60

Song of Songs, 79

Zechariah, 100, 102

Zephaniah, 90, 95